ANIMAL WISDOM

A GUIDED JOURNAL FOR CONNECTING WITH NATURE

VANESSA CHAKOUR

Illustrations by Thiago Bianchini

STERLING TEEN
New York

STERLING TEEN
New York

An Imprint of Sterling Publishing Co., Inc.

STERLING CHILDREN'S BOOKS and the distinctive Sterling Children's Books logo are registered trademarks of Sterling Publishing Co., Inc.

© 2021 Quarto Publishing plc

First Sterling edition published in 2021.

ISBN 978-1-4549-4225-2

Distributed in Canada by
Sterling Publishing Co., Inc.
c/o Canadian Manda Group,
664 Annette Street, Toronto,
Ontario M6S 2C8, Canada

For information about custom editions, special sales, and premium and corporate purchases, please contact Sterling Special Sales at 800-805-5489 or specialsales@sterlingpublishing.com.

CAUTION: The publisher and the author do not accept any liability or responsibility for any consequences caused by consuming and using any wild food relying upon the information or resources contained within this book.

Patterns from Shutterstock.com. Images: p28, p55: Katja Gerasimova/Shutterstock.com; pp111: Ecaterina Sciuchina/Shutterstock.com; p123: intueri/Shutterstock.com; p143: Tamiris6/Shutterstock.com.

Manufactured in China

2 4 6 8 10 9 7 5 3 1

05/21

sterlingpublishing.com

CONTENTS

Introduction	6
About this Book	8
Key Words	10
Ways to Connect with Your Animal Ally	12

1 *Animals of the Land* 14

Wolf	16
Snow Leopard	22
Black Bear	26
Orangutan	30
Rhinoceros	36
Spider	40
Red Squirrel	44
Elephant	48
Red Fox	54
Snake	60
Horse	66
Koala	70
Panda Bear	76
Tiger	80

2 Animals of the Water   *84*

Great White Shark   86
Seal   90
Octopus   96
Crab   100
Platypus   106
Marine Iguana   110
Dolphin   114
Seahorse   118
Humpback Whale   122
Tree Frog   128
Sea Otter   132
Turtle   136

3 Animals of the Air   *140*

Butterfly   142
Owl   146
Eagle   150
Hummingbird   154
Firefly   158
Bumblebee   162
Raven   166
Albatross   172
Bat   176
Dragonfly   180

International Organizations   184
Glossary   188
Index   190
Dedication   192

INTRODUCTION

For the last decade, I've worked on behalf of wolves, one of the most misunderstood and persecuted allies in our diverse animal kingdom. At first, I didn't know why I was so drawn to wolves, but as I learned more about their role in the environment as important ecological stewards, I realized that their purpose mirrors my own. Animals, with their sharp instincts and clear understanding of who they are, can be our teachers. There are times when we are ravenous like the shark, undergo profound metamorphosis like the butterfly, or weave our own destinies as we patiently wait for it all to unfold, like the spider. Other times, we may need to savor the sweetness of life like the bumblebee or reach out our hands for affection and connection like the sea otter. In these pages, we take a closer look at 36 incredible animals that share our planet and, in the process, come to understand more about ourselves.

Indigenous cultures knew, and continue to know, that we are but one part of a rich and biodiverse family of plants, animals, and fungi, inseparable from nature. The ancient Celts, Native Americans, ancient Egyptians, Siberian shamans, and others around the world looked to animals for guidance and a symbolic understanding of themselves and the natural world. But as people were separated from the land that carried their stories, and the Earth-based wisdom of their indigenous and Earth-centered cultures, many forgot how much we depend

upon, and can learn from, our clawed, furred, and feathered family. This book aims to remind, reconnect, and engage you. The wisdom of wild animals is timeless and in this period of ecological crisis, they desperately need us to heed the call of the wild and to listen. At a time when climate change, deforestation, and pollution are having such an adverse impact on wildlife the world over—with more and more animals listed on the International Union for Conservation of Nature's Red List of Threatened Species— now is the moment for each of us to do all we can to protect the natural world.

Every wild animal is clear about the role they play in our beautiful, wild world, and they have much to teach us and remind us about our own.

It is an honor to share these magnificent creatures with you. May they guide and inspire you for years to come.

Vanessa

ABOUT THIS BOOK

There is no right or wrong way to use this book, so I encourage you to trust your instincts, use your imagination, and explore. You may find there are animals that speak deeply to you; they might appear in your night-time dreams or you may suddenly see them repeatedly in the outside world. Listen to those cues and find the animal or their closest relative in this book. Connecting with animal guides can heighten your instinct and be a window to your unique purpose within your inner and outer worlds.

There are other times when you may be seeking guidance. In those instances, I suggest you close your eyes and ask a question, or simply tune in to your intuition and open the book to a page with your non-dominant hand. Trust that your inner knowing will guide you to the creature that has a message for you. Or, you may also want to use the key words listed on pages 10–11 to see which ones resonate with you on that given day, and then turn to that animal for guidance and inspiration. As you learn more about each mammal, reptile, fish, or insect, you will find suggestions for various practices and activities. Do those that call to you, picking and choosing the ones you like best.

Then, I encourage you to take your creative inspiration and relationship with your animal ally into the world, sharing their magic with others. Since animals can't speak in the ways that we can, they need us to communicate on their behalf. We can make the world a kinder and more harmonious place by educating each other and creating more beauty all around us.

Each chapter contains a selection of animal profiles that will speak to an aspect of who you are and deliver a message that will awaken your inner wisdom. Learn about the history, purpose, and culture surrounding these animals.

WOLF

Ecological Stewardship • Wildness • Family

"If the wolf has come into your life, it may be time to learn what it means to be a steward of your local ecosystem."

You'll find ways to connect with the animal through activities, movement, meditation, and more. Learn more about this on pages 12–13.

Allow the interactive prompts to strengthen your relationship with yourself and with the natural world. Use the space provided to journal, sketch, or let the creative juices flow in other ways.

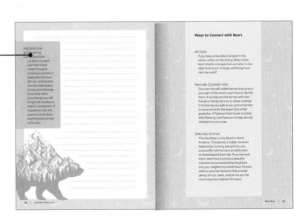

Key Words

Animal	Characteristics
Wolf	Ecological Stewardship • Wildness • Family
Snow leopard	Strength • Elegance • Elusiveness
Black bear	Nurturing • Hibernation • Introspection
Orangutan	Peace • Presence • Solitude
Rhinoceros	Tranquility • Tenacity • Groundedness
Spider	Creativity • Receptivity • Patience
Red squirrel	Energy • Athleticism • Preparedness
Elephant	Kindness • Ancient Wisdom • Cooperation
Red fox	Adaptability • Intelligence • Ingenuity
Snake	Transcendence • Rebirth • Renewal
Horse	Dedication • Endurance • Grace
Koala	Comfort • Affection • Specificity
Panda bear	Sacred Space • Balance • Harmony
Tiger	Power • Confidence • Dignity
Great white shark	Relentlessness • Hunger • Focus
Seal	Balance • Longing • Inner Voice
Octopus	Mystery • Intuition • Ingenuity
Crab	Rhythm • Protection • Sensitivity

If you're unsure which animal to turn to, I invite you to use the table below, feel the words that resonate with you, and read about that animal ally. You can also close your eyes, take a deep breath, and use your finger to scroll down the page. Stop when your instinct says so. As you find yourself in need of guidance in the following days, weeks, or months, you may want to explore these exercises again.

Animal	*Characteristics*
Platypus	Unique • Unpredictable • Enigmatic
Marine iguana	Adaptability • Meditative Stillness • Depth
Dolphin	Communication • Cooperation • Compassion
Seahorse	Awareness • Partnership • Patience
Humpback whale	Consciousness • Mystery • Soul Song
Tree frog	Song • New Beginnings • Transformation
Sea otter	Affection • Cooperation • Play
Turtle	Mindfulness • Sagacity • Slowing Down
Owl	Navigation • Presence • Inner Knowing
Eagle	Confidence • Intensity • Perspective
Hummingbird	Joy • Radiance • Remembrance
Bumblebee	Sweetness • Attraction • Devotion
Raven	Mystery • Confidence • Esoteric Wisdom
Albatross	Endurance • Loyalty • Partnership
Bat	Acute Perception • Initiation • Rebirth
Butterfly	Change • Trust • Letting Go
Firefly	Inner Spark • Magic • Wonder
Dragonfly	Imagination • Vision • Transcendence

Ways to Connect
with Your Animal Ally

The practices in this workbook offer ways to engage your imagination, deepen your relationship with nature, get involved in environmental conservation, and nurture your wellbeing.

Movement to embrace your body and awaken your instinctive self

Conscious movement can increase your vitality while stimulating energy, ideas, and understanding. These practices invite you to embody your animal self by mimicking the graceful gait of the fox or the regal strength of the tiger. You may want to watch videos of how your creature crawls, buzzes, slithers, stares, or leaps, and (safely and mindfully) mimic them. If the suggested movement isn't possible for you, close your eyes and channel your animal ally through your breath and move in subtle ways that inspire you.

Meditation and mindfulness practices

Meditation is a way to still incessant thoughts and come closer to the present-moment pulse of life. You'll find different meditative and mindfulness practices in these pages—from visualization exercises to short sessions of silent meditation that offer ways to step into the perspective of your animal ally. You might explore a slower, more mindful pace like the tortoise, the big-picture perspective of the hawk, or the heightened awareness of the snow leopard. Sensing through the eyes and ears of these animals can help broaden your perspective, look at the challenges in your life through a different lens, and awaken to the wonders of nature.

Species status and awareness

Habitat loss is one of the greatest causes of species extinction worldwide, and for every habitat we lose, we eliminate a stronghold for countless plant and animal species. In the back of the book, you'll find a list of organizations that work on behalf of wild animals and the landscapes they depend upon. This is a tool and a resource to help you learn, get involved, and make a difference.

Creative, sensory, and inner exploration through writing, journaling, and drawing to peel back the layers and find the real you

These are practices that help you engage your imagination and explore the infinite possibilities of your creativity. Some exercises include stream-of-consciousness journaling, writing your own fairy tale, or drawing from within. The practice of free-form journaling or drawing can help get things out of your system, while other approaches can help you develop more intimacy with nature through keen observation of the world around you. It can be interesting to explore writing or drawing with your non-dominant hand. Using a different side of our body taps into a different side of our mind. With some subtle changes to the creative practices in this book, you can go back to them again and again to uncover more about yourself and your unique gifts. There is always more to discover.

Nature connection to heal and build your relationship with your animal self

As you learn to identify and name the incredible plants and animals that surround you, you will deepen your relationship with the environment. This growing awareness can awaken your wonder. Some of these practices include learning how to identify local trees and plants, or the flowers that essential pollinators like hummingbirds and bumblebees like to visit. As you learn, you will understand what can be done to make the world a more habitable and beautiful place.

Actions and activities

These activities invite you to play an active role in healing the environment. From challenging yourself to creating zero waste to planting flowers for pollinators, these exercises invite you to make the world a healthier and more beautiful place for everyone.

Dreamwork to awaken what may be hidden underneath the realm of your conscious awareness

We spend an estimated one-third of our lives sleeping, and as we do, we dream. Many cultures and traditions use insight from dreams to become more self-aware. It is with this in mind that you are invited to explore the realm of your dreams. Animal allies like the owl might help you navigate darkness and shadows, while sea creatures like the humpback whale or marine iguana can dive into your watery emotional realms and subconscious depths. I encourage you to keep a dream journal and write down the feelings and the images from your dreams when you wake up.

Creatures who crawl, leap, run, slither, and gallop upon the Earth. Connect with your instincts as you learn about animals like the fox, horse, wolf, bear, snake, and spider.

1 ANIMALS OF THE LAND

WOLF

Ecological Stewardship • Wildness • Family

Though many have to come to know the wolf as the predatory villain in tales like "Little Red Riding Hood," this is far from their true nature. Wolf packs are tight-knit families, each with their own history, unique skill sets, and traditions. Indigenous cultures that practiced a hunter-gatherer way of life recognized our tribal similarities and respected wolves as spiritual and intelligent creatures. In most Native American tribes, the wolf is associated with courage, strength, loyalty, and wisdom. In Shoshone mythology, the wolf plays the role of Creator god, while in Anishinaabe mythology a wolf known as Ma'iingan is brother to Original Man. In Celtic mythology, wolves were companions of Moon goddesses such as Cerridwen, and in Scottish Gaelic, the name for wolf is *Mac Tire*, meaning "son of the countryside."

However, as societies became more domesticated, people's relationship with the land changed, and fear and misunderstanding of wolves grew so strong that they were hunted to the brink of extinction. Luckily, conservationists have worked hard to educate the public and help people remember the true role of wolves as stewards of an ecosystem. When wolves were reintroduced to Yellowstone National Park in 1995 after a 70-year absence, they transformed the land and helped increase biodiversity. They were brought in to manage a rising elk population, which had been overgrazing much of the park, but their impact went far beyond that. The presence of the wolves changed the elks' behavior and in turn, the park's rivers and forests began to recover. This provided increased habitat for other animals such as eagles, beavers, and bison who began to increase in numbers and, in some cases, return. If the wolf has come into your life, it may be time to learn what it means to be a steward of your local environment. The wolf invites us to build strong networks and bonds for the greater good, while teaching and guiding those who misunderstand.

"*If the wolf has come into your life, it may be time to learn what it means to be a steward of your local ecosystem.*"

Ways to Connect with Wolves

SPECIES STATUS

There are two universally recognized species of wolves in the world: the gray wolf (*Canis lupus*) and the red wolf (*Canis rufus*). The red wolf is the world's most endangered mammal in the Canidae family, which also includes foxes and coyotes. A wildlife refuge in eastern North Carolina is the only place they exist in the wild and there are now less than 20 wild wolves. The Wolf Conservation Center in New York is one of 40 organizations that take part in the Species Survival Program to help to keep the red wolf alive

NATURE CONNECTION

Wolves are stewards of their environment. What does the term "ecological steward" mean to you? How can you help to bring more balance and biodiversity to your local ecosystem?

ACTIVITIES

Howl at the Moon!

Share the true story of wolves with those around you, so that your friends and family can revise their stories too, and perhaps get involved in their protection.

INNER EXPLORATION

Have you ever felt
misunderstood?
Write about it here
and, if possible,
explore how you
might communicate
with others in the
future to change how
they perceive you.

CREATIVE WRITING

Revise the story of the Big Bad Wolf—writing the story with the wolf as the hero.

SNOW LEOPARD

Strength · Elegance · Elusiveness

Snow leopards are beautiful and elusive felines native to the Himalayan mountain ranges of Central and South Asia. Known as the "gray ghost of the mountains," these large cats reside on cold, steep cliffs where their wide, fur-covered feet act as natural snowshoes and their long tails can wrap around their bodies like blankets. Their thick, patterned coats help them blend into the rocky slopes, and though their markings may look similar, they are as unique as our fingerprints. Camouflage can be necessary for us too when we feel out of our element or over-exposed, and like the snow leopard we can use clever means of disguise to move in the background. Like other felines, snow leopards have finely tuned senses that enable them to hunt in darkness, but unlike the other big felines, the snow leopard is unable to roar and instead hisses, growls, puffs, yowls, and purrs.

Some locals describe snow leopards as important boundary keepers and protectors of crops, since without them, livestock would be free to range and overgraze fields.

These magical creatures live most of their lives in solitude in high mountain peaks, which aligns them with the mystical, magical aspects of our nature. If the snow leopard appears, you may benefit from solitary time to help you gain perspective, travel to new heights, and see more clearly.

"If the snow leopard appears, you may benefit from solitary time to help you gain perspective, travel to new heights, and see more clearly."

Ways to Connect with Snow Leopards

SPECIES STATUS

Habitat loss poses a significant threat to the snow leopard. Climate change is increasing the altitude of the tree line, diminishing the range of these big cats and their prey. This is shrinking the leopard's habitat and reducing the abundance of wild prey for them to feed on, making the cat increasingly reliant on livestock for survival.

ACTION

Climate change is the largest, underlying threat for snow leopards. In honor of the snow leopard, adopt or eliminate one habit to reduce greenhouse gases—perhaps start carrying a cloth bag with you, instead of using a plastic one, or use only recyclable paper for drawing, printing, or when wrapping gifts.

MOVEMENT

Channel the snow leopard while hiking up your nearest hill and spend some time at the top to gain clarity and perspective. Reflect upon how you can express yourself with honesty.

MEDITATION

Use visualization to imagine climbing a high, snowy peak with the snow leopard as your companion. Let yourself be taken on a journey and journal about what you discover together.

BLACK BEAR

Nurturing · Hibernation · Introspection

The bear helps us navigate the two states of introspection and action. Black bears enter their dens for months of hibernation in late fall and emerge in spring ravenous and focused on finding food. Because of this ebb and flow, many ancient peoples associated the black bear with the waxing and waning of the Moon.

Though bears have a calm and playful exterior, there is an explosive power surging just beneath the surface, especially when it comes to the defense of their young. A skillful mother, the mother bear cares for her young with absolute devotion. Since bears can walk upright and forage for berries, roots, and leaves, they were symbols of wisdom and medicine for many Native American tribes. If one dreamt about the bear, they would soon walk the path of the healer.

Black bears have better eyesight and hearing than humans and an incredible sense of smell. They regularly climb trees to feed or escape from harm, and those fortunate to have bodies of water nearby will swim for pleasure. These animals remind us to enjoy life and to savor the bounty we are given by the Earth. Bears ask you to rest and enter the caves of your unconscious so that deep longings can emerge. When you wake up you'll know what you are truly hungry for.

"If one dreamt about the bear, they would soon walk the path of the healer."

MEDITATION & CREATIVE EXPLORATION

Lie down in a dark room and travel inward. Imagine entering a cave for a designated amount of time, and breathe into that dark space to rest and recharge. Know that when you emerge you will bring forth newfound wisdom and sparks of inspiration. Use this space to write down anything that comes up for you.

Ways to Connect with Bears

ACTION

If you have a new idea or project in the works, reflect on the timing. When is the best time for introspection and when is the ideal time to act, emerge, and bring it out into the world?

NATURE CONNECTION

Discover the wild, edible berries that grow in your part of the world. Learn how to identify them. If you harvest the berries with your friends or family, be sure to check carefully if the berries are safe to eat, and remember to leave some for the bears! Get a field guide like, *A Peterson Field Guide to Edible Wild Plants* by Lee Peterson to help identify wild plants in your area.

SPECIES STATUS

The black bear is only found in North America. The species is stable; however, habitat loss, hunting, being hit by cars, and conflict with humans are all threats to these beautiful animals. If you live near them, learn how to practice peaceful coexistence and avoid attracting bears into your neighborhood with food. Forests without a human footprint that provide plenty of nuts, barks, and berries are the most important habitats for bears.

ORANGUTAN

Peace · Presence · Solitude

The word *orangutan* means "person of the forest" in the Malay and Indonesian languages. These close relatives call upon us to slow down and to reflect upon our humanity and role within the web of life. Indigenous cultures like the Iban people of Indonesia that live among orangutans revere these primates as reincarnations of respected members of their community and tell tales about orangutans saving their loved ones from disaster. For the Iban tribe, nature is inseparable from culture, so they revere and protect this wild kin.

Orangutans share 97 percent of our DNA and are found only in the rain forests of the Southeast Asian islands of Borneo and Sumatra. They are highly intelligent and peaceful mammals, spending most of their lives swinging in tree tops, feasting on wild fruits, and drinking water from holes in trees. Unlike other primates, orangutans lead solitary lives once they reach maturity. They venture off at about 8 years old after experiencing a close relationship with their mothers who carry them on their backs for the first 5 years of their lives. Orangutan mothers give birth to a baby every 8-10 years, starting at the age of 17 and raising them on their own. Orangutans can live to be about 60 years old. If this animal shows up for you, consider spending some time in solitude and reflecting upon what matters most.

"If this animal shows up for you, consider spending some time in solitude and reflecting upon what matters most."

Ways to Connect with Orangutans

Action & Awareness

Be aware and read labels carefully. One of the biggest threats to orangutans is the production of palm oil which has devastated their habitat. Palm oil is in countless processed food products like chips, crackers, cookies, and candy. Do some research, and limit your consumption of products that contain palm oil. Share this information with others, so they can also protect this peaceful being.

Species Status

Orangutans are categorized as Critically Endangered on the IUCN Red List of Threatened Species. This peaceful wild relative is threatened with extinction due to massive deforestation for pulp paper and palm oil plantations.

Nature Connection

If you can, take a walk in a forest and imagine orangutans climbing and building nests in the trees. Reflect on your own relationship with the forest.

MEDITATION

Carve out at least an hour to spend alone this week. If you can, sit near a tree that calls to you, then meditate and reflect on what matters most to you. Journal about what you feel and find within.

CREATIVE EXPLORATION

Orangutans are better protected in areas where stories about our kinship are told, as with the Iban people. This goes to show how the power of belief and story affects our relationship with the wild. Spend some time learning more about this close kin and write a story.

RHINOCEROS

Tranquility · Tenacity · Groundedness

The rhinoceros is one of the Earth's largest mammals, and while they may look intimidating, these ancient creatures are gentle herbivores. Rhinos have been around for millions of years and play a crucial role in their grassland ecosystem as important grazers. They are a keystone species whose presence promotes biodiversity. The African species of rhinoceros lacks teeth at the front of their mouths, so they rely on their lips to pluck grasses. The Sumatran rhino is a browser whose favorite foods include plant tips, twigs, and fruits. They are the smallest and hairiest of all surviving rhinos and can trace their lineage all the way back to the Ice Age. They communicate with whistling and whining noises, and leave a network of scented trails in order to find one another.

Rhinoceroses are known for their distinguishing horns made of keratin, the same type of protein that makes up hair and fingernails. Sadly, some people believe that ingesting the horn has health benefits (this is untrue), and this has pushed these peaceful creatures to the brink of extinction. They use their strong horns to dig in dry, compacted soil for water and roots when either is scarce. They also use their horns to intimidate others and, when necessary, defend territory. If you come upon the rhinoceros, it is a message that an intimidating situation may not be what it seems.

"If you come upon the rhinoceros, it is a message that an intimidating situation may not be what it seems."

Ways to Connect with Rhinoceroses

ACTIVITIES

Learn about the keystone species in your environment (see page 189). Who is thriving and who is missing? What impact does their presence or absence have on the land?

SPECIES STATUS

The IUCN Red List of Threatened Species identifies the Black, Javan, and Sumatran rhinoceros as Critically Endangered. There are less than 80 Sumatran rhinos left in the wild. Historically, poaching depleted the population, but their biggest threat today is habitat loss from forest destruction for palm oil and paper pulp, and increasingly, small, fragmented populations that make it difficult for them to find a partner and have offspring. Africa's white rhinos are divided into two subspecies: northern and southern. While the southern subspecies is in fairly good shape, the northern rhino has been driven to extinction in the wild.

ACTION

Be mindful of your purchases. Some shampoos, beauty products, and soaps use palm oil which threatens the Sumatran rhinoceros. If you must buy a product containing the oil, then make sure it is certified sustainable palm oil (CSPO). Donate, volunteer, and raise awareness of this ancient species. See page 184 for a list of organizations.

MEDITATION

Meditate on a situation that has been intimidating you with the intention of exploring new ways of looking at it. Set a designated amount of time to ground yourself through deep breaths and invite the rhino to accompany you. Walk around all sides of the challenge together until you find a new level of understanding. Journal about what you discover.

SPIDER

Creativity · Receptivity · Patience

As the weaver of webs, the spider symbolizes the spirit of creation. These patient and skilled creators belong to a group of animals called arachnids whose scientific name is derived from Arachne, a talented weaver in Greek mythology who was transformed into a spider when she angered Athena.

These creatures are incredible artisans that weave intricate webs, which appear to be delicate, but are incredibly resilient. The only reason we can break spider webs is that they are so thin, but in reality the material is stronger than steel. Spiders have a special gland on their abdomen that produces this magical silk, which they can use to climb from plant to plant and create cocoons, traps, and incredible ballooning lines. Sometimes called kiting, ballooning is a process by which spiders move through the air by releasing one or more of their threads to catch the wind. In order to do so, a spider climbs to a high point, tests the direction of the wind, and if the breeze is right, they lift their abdomen to the sky, releasing fine silk threads until they float away.

Webs are the life and home of the female spider—where they live, eat, and breed all their lives. That's why they put so much effort into constructing a strong and beautiful web—their food and mates come to them. Females are bigger and stronger, and typically stay in one place throughout their lives. Males, on the other hand, are smaller, have to travel a lot, and they may even be eaten by their mate. Life is harder for the male spider. While young male spiders might build webs to catch prey, they abandon them when they go out looking for a mate. Abandoned, and often sloppy, these temporary structures become cobwebs.

The presence of the spider asks you to confront unfounded fears and show patience with a creative project or idea that you are trying to realize. When the spider crawls into your life, you are being asked to look at the power of small things. Creations that appear delicate, and almost invisible, might actually have incredible resilience.

"When the spider crawls into your life, you are being asked to look at the power of small things. Creations that appear delicate, and almost invisible, might actually have incredible resilience."

Ways to Connect with Spiders

SENSORY EXPLORATION

Explore your spidey senses. A spider's most important source of information about the world comes from highly sensitive hairs that cover most of their body. These hairs perceive even low-level vibrations coming through any surface that a spider stands on. Explore your own sense perceptions through sound and vibration.

SPECIES STATUS

There are more than 45,000 known species of spiders, found in habitats all over the world.

ACTIVITIES

Explore the art of weaving using a hand loom or through creating a piece of art inspired by the spider's web. Is there a project you've abandoned that is collecting dust? Is it time to revisit it or clear it away?

ACTION

The most common creature-based phobia in the world is arachnophobia, the fear of spiders, but house spiders are generally harmless and feed on common indoor pests like flies and cockroaches. If left alone, they can provide effective home pest control. Learn about the spiders in your local area to overcome any fear and maybe even learn to appreciate these amazing creatures.

Use this space to
draw a spider's web.
Add any unfounded
fears to the web,
so you can trap and
confront them.

Red Squirrel

Energy · Athleticism · Preparedness

Squirrels have boundless energy and are always gathering food and preparing for the future. We see them stocking up on nuts for uncertain times and cold winter days ahead. They hide caches of food in and near their nests so they are ready for almost anything, and while they work hard and always seem to be busy, they are also playful. They run and jump among branches, and also have a trickster quality because they dig holes and fill them in without leaving any food behind to throw other animals off their trail. Red squirrels are sometimes called "pine squirrels" since they are mainly found in mature coniferous forests and favor pine nuts. Unlike their cousin, the tenacious gray squirrel that can thrive in urban areas, red squirrels depend on woodlands to survive. They are specially adapted to feed on the seeds in pine cones, which makes them important for the regeneration of pine forests.

Squirrels communicate their emotional states in a number of different ways—they might growl, grind their teeth, and use clicks and squeaks while stamping their feet or twitching their tails. Red squirrels are significantly smaller than their cousin, the gray, but they make up for that with attitude. If you have offended a red squirrel, they will let you know. They might position themselves on a branch high above you while they yell, chatter, and wag their tail, giving you a piece of their mind. The primary message a squirrel sends with their wagging tail is a warning. If they see something dangerous or suspicious, they use their tails to alert other squirrels. They also use their tail to let predators know they've seen the danger, informing them that they will not be fooled by the element of surprise.

A small creature, with a big personality, the red squirrel reminds us to speak our mind if important boundaries have been crossed. They remind us to be diligent in gathering what we need, so we are ready, whatever comes our way. If a squirrel crosses your path while you are working toward an important goal, they are telling you to stick with it but not to forget to have fun in the process.

"*If a squirrel crosses your path while you are working toward an important goal, they are telling you to stick with it but not to forget to have fun in the process.*"

Ways to Connect with Red Squirrels

MOVEMENT

Join a climbing center and learn how to scramble upward quickly, just like the squirrel.

MEDITATION

Walk in a nearby pine forest or sit under a pine tree to meditate. Is something coming up that you need to prepare for, such as a test or a job interview? Engage the energy of the squirrel to be ready, through research and organization.

SPECIES STATUS

American red squirrels can be found throughout the United States in coniferous forests. The population of red squirrels in the United Kingdom has decreased due to deforestation and the introduction of the eastern gray squirrel.

ACTION

Get involved in planting trees, preserving old-growth pine forests, and reforestation.

ACTIVITY

Red squirrels have a strong symbiotic relationship with the pine tree. Learn how to identify the species of pine trees and other evergreens around you. Use this space to draw their needles, cones and other key characteristics.

ELEPHANT

Kindness · Ancient Wisdom · Cooperation

Elephants are known for their compassionate and altruistic treatment of each other. They are loyal to and will defend their friends and family. If one member of an elephant herd is injured, others will risk their lives to get them back to safety. These majestic animals remind us of the power of love and loyalty to our friends, relatives, and chosen family.

The African elephant is the world's largest land animal and can be found in savannas, forests, and woodlands of the continent. As the largest of all land mammals, African elephants play an important role in balancing natural ecosystems. They trample dense grasslands and create water holes that can be used by other wildlife when rainfall is low. African lore suggests that elephants are reincarnated from ancient human chiefs, as their role is to create harmony and settle disputes among other wild creatures. Asian elephants can be found in the forests of India and Southeast Asia, and are slightly smaller than their African cousins.

When the elephant comes into your life, they are calling on you to reflect upon your connectedness to friends, family, and your local environment. Do you have strong bonds? If the answer is no, you are being summoned to strengthen them. With the help of the elephant, it is time to deepen existing connections and share your gratitude with those around you.

"When the elephant comes into your life, they are calling on you to reflect upon your connectedness to friends, family, and your local environment."

Ways to Connect with Elephants

Nature Connection

Channel the kindness of the elephant and go for a nature walk with those you love. As you walk, practice compassion for the creatures in your environment by picking up litter and taking note of any wild areas that might need support.

Species Status

These gentle, wild animals have been exploited in circuses, and continue to be used for our entertainment but, thankfully, more and more places are releasing elephants from this cruel humiliation. These intelligent and kind animals deserve to live in the wild, with their beloved tribe. Today, they struggle under constant threat from habitat loss, human-wildlife conflict, and poaching for ivory. Sumatran elephants are Critically Endangered on the IUCN Red List of Threatened Species and an estimated 35,000 African elephants are killed every year for their tusks. The natural increase of these elephant populations has yet to overtake the rate of killing.

ACTION

Support and engage with elephant conservation organizations. Write letters to your local leaders, and get involved in any way you can in order to prevent the exploitation of this wise and compassionate animal. If you're raising money for an organization, use the table below to track how much you have collected.

Goal: _____

Date	Amount

CREATIVE EXPLORATION

Take some time to reflect on your friends and your family. Is there someone who consistently comes to your aid when you need it? Meditate on your own pack of supporters and use the space provided here to make a gratitude list of all the people who have been there for you. Afterward, you may want to send letters or thank you cards in the mail to express your gratitude and strengthen your bonds. Use the space on the opposite page to draft your thank you note.

Red Fox

Adaptability · Intelligence · Ingenuity

The red fox has stirred our imagination for centuries as a key character in fairy tales. While some stories portray the fox as a faithful guardian, friend, or lover, most tell tales of trickery and deceit. The fox has been hunted for sport and subject to inhumane treatment in fur farms but, despite human threats, this intelligent creature thrives among us in many suburban and urban areas. Their natural habitats include forests, mountains, and deserts, and their diet is just as flexible, as they eat everything from fruit to scavenged scraps.

The term "foxy" implies a wild sensuality. In folklore, fox wives or vixens are seductive creatures who entice unwary travelers with their mysterious beauty. In some tales, they drain men of vital energy, while in others, they are kind but can't be tamed. Fox men also seduce those who are lost with charm and trickery. The fox's fiery coat has also played a part in stories; their flamelike tails and ability to adapt are often identified with shapeshifting and fire.

If the red fox comes into your life, it may be time to embrace your wild self. The fox lives on the edge of our domesticated worlds, calling upon us to remember and rewild. Reflect upon your personal narrative. How has your personal story impacted your life? With the help of the fiery fox, you might ignite a more feral and free version of your own fairy tale.

> *"If the red fox comes into your life, it may be time to embrace your wild self."*

Ways to Connect with Foxes

MOVEMENT

If you need to ignite or focus a scattered inner flame, explore a martial art. If you need to calm your inner fire, try a yoga class or something equally soothing.

NATURE CONNECTION

Go for a walk in a new natural environment or simply walk down a different path. Channel the fox and notice how your senses adapt, what stands out for you, and how the new setting may shift your perspective.

SPECIES STATUS

Though the red fox population is stable, they are still subject to the cruelty of fur farms and hunting for sport. Refer to the back of the book for organizations or sanctuaries that rescue foxes. If this is your animal ally, get involved in their protection.

ACTIVITIES

Learn more about the fox and the way they communicate with each other. Listen to their calls and try to mimic them.

MEDITATION

Sit with your eyes open and stare in one place like a fox on the hunt. Set a designated period of time and breathe into your solar plexus to tap into your inner fire. Afterward, write about or draw what you feel. Do you need to ignite or focus your inner flame?

CREATIVE EXPLORATION

Read folklore such as "The Foxwife" and journal about what comes up for you. Write a story about yourself as the fox or a new fairy tale about your life.

SNAKE

Transcendence · Rebirth · Renewal

Snakes symbolize transformation, healing, and renewal. If the snake comes up for you, it might be time to shed layers that you've outgrown. When a snake is ready to molt, their old skin becomes dull and their eyes go cloudy, as though they have entered a trance. They stop eating, move to a safe space, and after a few days of molting, their eyes clear and they emerge from their old skin completely renewed. This teaches us to let go of thoughts, patterns, or external influences that are dulling our mind, body, or spirit. In some cases, we might need to retreat as we endure a period of change.

Snakes have been sacred to many cultures throughout the world as symbols of healing. The most familiar image may be the Rod of Asclepius, the Greek God of medicine. In yogic traditions the snake represents Kundalini, the life force or energy coiled at the base of the spine, which lies dormant until a person awakens. The Ouroboros, which originated in ancient Egypt, is the alchemical symbol of a serpent eating its own tail. It is interpreted as a symbol of the cycle of life, death, and rebirth. Though many people are fearful of snakes, they play an important role in our ecosystem, maintaining balance in the web of life.

"If the snake comes up for you, it might be time to shed layers that you've outgrown."

CREATIVE EXPLORATION

Use this prompt and give yourself a designated amount of time to free-write: "I am ready to shed…" Draw or create a collage of images showing your old skins. Honor your past experiences as you let go of them.

Ways to Connect with Snakes

Movement & Meditation

Move your spine back and forth and reflect on its structure. Do you feel stiff or flexible? Stretch and move until your spine feels fluid and graceful, just like the movement of a snake.

Species Status

There are about 3,500 known snake species. Many of them are classified as Critically Endangered or Vulnerable on the IUCN Red List of Threatened Species.

Nature Connection

Learn about the snakes in your local area and their role in the ecosystem.

ACTION

Go through old clothes and other material items and see what you've outgrown or no longer need. Make a list and then donate these to charity in order to declutter and create more space around you.

HORSE

Dedication · Endurance · Grace

These beautiful animals symbolize true dedication. Horse whisperers knew, and continue to know, how to communicate with this animal's unbridled nature while peacefully building trust and intimate bonds. Others, without the patience and talent for communication, believed they had to use cruelty to "break" a horse to subdue their wild spirit into submission. Horses have accompanied humans through wars, enabled us to travel and move goods, and helped us to plant and harvest food quickly and easily. They have been faithful companions for centuries, being our first forms of transportation on land and giving us the ability to explore and feel free.

The Celts hailed horses as beasts belonging to the Sun god, and assigned them a place with the goddess Epona. In the wild, horses live in herds led by a mature male called a stallion. Domesticated horses were introduced into North America at the time of the Spanish conquest in the 16th century, and escaped horses subsequently spread throughout the American Great Plains and became feral.

If the horse comes into your life, it may be time to speak to your own unbridled nature, and reflect on those aspects of your wild soul that you may have taken for granted. It is time to whisper to your inner longings so you can work together to feel free.

"If the horse comes into your life, it may be time to speak to your own unbridled nature, and reflect on those aspects of your wild soul that you may have taken for granted."

MEDITATION

We are often obsessed these days with getting somewhere as fast as possible. While there are still people in the world who travel by horse, they are mainly used for recreation or in sport rather than for transportation. Take some time to slow down as you walk, bike, or drive. Do you really need to speed through life? What's the rush?

SPECIES STATUS

Since horses have been domesticated for centuries, it may be hard to think of them as the wild creatures they once were. The Faeroese pony, found on the Faeroe Islands between Iceland and the Shetland Islands, is one of the oldest breeds of horses. This breed is rare and, in fact, almost extinct. The Przewalski's horse, the only true wild horse, is listed as Critically Endangered on the IUCN Red List of Threatened Species. The Chincoteague ponies, also known as the Assateague horses, were once domesticated horses that now live wild lives on Assateague Island in Virginia and Maryland. Evidence suggests that these feral horses are the descendants of survivors from a Spanish galleon that crashed off the coast of Assateague.

ACTION

If possible, visit horses in your area. Get involved with organizations that work on their behalf, teaching people to whisper to them and finding ways to protect those horses remaining in the wild.

INNER EXPLORATION

How do you work with your own vital energy? Do you whisper to it and get to know it so you can form a close relationship? Or is it an unwilling and fearful partnership? Explore your inner dialogue and see if you can be kinder to yourself as you steer in the directions you want to go. Use this space to write a few life affirmations.

KOALA

Comfort · Affection · Specificity

Koalas live in the eucalyptus forests of southeastern and eastern Australia. Known for their cuddly and calm nature, these adorable animals have an intimate relationship with the eucalyptus tree which they depend on as a source of food and as a home. Koalas have sharp claws that allow them to hold on tight to branches. The koala's digestive system has to work hard to break down the toxins and extract limited nutrients from their narrow diet of eucalyptus. With little energy from their diet, they may sleep up to 18 hours a day. Koalas eat so much eucalyptus that they often take on the menthol-like smell of the plant.

Like kangaroos, koalas are marsupials with pouches where their babies develop. Newborn koalas, called joeys, are only about the size of a bumblebee and are born blind, hairless, and without ears. Koalas need a lot of space—about a hundred trees per animal—which has become a devastating problem as Australia's woodlands continue to shrink. Land clearing, logging, and bushfires have destroyed much of the forest koalas depend on. In response to droughts, koalas are forced to stop napping and come down from trees to find water, using precious energy and putting themselves at a higher risk of predation. If the koala has shown up for you, it is a calling to rest, reflect, and remember the importance of the simple things in life.

"If the koala has shown up for you, it is a calling to rest, reflect, and remember the importance of the simple things in life."

CREATIVE EXPLORATION

Find a eucalyptus tree nearby or look for a picture of one online. Use this space to make a sketch of the tree, adding koalas as you go.

Ways to Connect with Koalas

ACTIVITY

Eucalyptus is often used as a decongestant in steam inhalation. The plant is included in many over-the-counter products such as mouthwash, vapor rub, and bug-repellant. Explore the uses of eucalyptus and, like the koala, become familiar with the scent and properties of the tree.

SPECIES STATUS

These animals desperately need our help. The IUCN Red List of Threatened Species has named koalas as one of 10 animals that are most vulnerable to climate change. Increasing carbon dioxide in the atmosphere has been shown to decrease the nutritional quality of eucalyptus leaves. It also causes longer and more intense droughts and wildfires which diminish their vital habitat.

ACTION

Plant trees and get involved in reforestation schemes where you live. Share the plight of the koala with others and donate to organizations working to protect these animals and their precious habitat.

INNER EXPLORATION

Reflect on the vulnerability of the koala and their special relationship with the eucalyptus tree. Is there something that you can't live without? Imagine if that was taken away. Journal about what that would feel like, and then write a list of what you are most grateful for.

I AM MOST GRATEFUL FOR...

★ _____

★ _____

★ _____

★ _____

★ _____

★ _____

★ _____

★ _____

★ _____

★ _____

★ _____

★ _____

PANDA BEAR

Sacred Space · Balance · Harmony

Panda bears live high in the mountains of Southwest China where they live peaceful and solitary lives for most of their existence. The panda's diet consists almost exclusively of bamboo, and they have lived in bamboo forests for millions of years. They are known to be shy and have docile temperaments, but as mothers, they are extremely protective and will burst into a rage if anyone comes close to their young. Under their soft and cuddly appearance, these bears show the importance of having strong personal boundaries to feel safe and grounded in life. Pandas are extremely sensitive to their surroundings and can quickly become stressed when there is too much movement or noise.

Though they spend most of their days lounging and eating bamboo, these bears are also agile climbers and proficient swimmers. They take shelter in hollow trees or rock crevices, but do not establish permanent dens. For this reason, pandas do not hibernate like other bears and will move to higher elevations with warmer temperatures. In Eastern cultures, pandas symbolize calm, a balance of opposites, and the harmonious resolution of conflict. If the panda shows up in your life, it is time to reflect on your sources of comfort in order to nurture yourself or others more mindfully. It is also a call to create some sacred space and protect what is vulnerable and most precious.

> *"If the panda shows up in your life, it is time to reflect on your sources of comfort in order to nurture yourself or others more mindfully."*

Ways to Connect with Pandas

ACTION

Donate to a charitable organization that protects pandas, along with conservation projects in China. Be aware of where and how your paper is sourced. Bamboo trees are being cut down to make paper products, destroying the panda's natural habitat and main food source. Choose recycled paper products when they are available, and always recycle these when you have finished using them.

MEDITATION

The solitude and serenity of panda bears remind us how important it is to feel at ease with ourselves, whether we are alone or with others. Try to set aside a few minutes each day for silence and contemplation for at least three weeks, and if you already enjoy meditating on a regular basis, reflect on ways you might deepen the experience.

SPECIES STATUS

As a result of farming, deforestation, and other human development, the giant panda has been driven out of the lowland areas where they once lived. In 2016, the IUCN Red List of Threatened Species reclassified the species from Endangered to Vulnerable. It is now estimated that there are only 1,864 pandas left in the wild.

ACTIVITY

It is important to have spaces where we feel calm, safe, and at ease. How do you feel in your inner and outer environment? Take time to create your own sacred space, perhaps displaying photographs of loved ones or your favorite places in the world. Make a list here of items that have a personal meaning or that help calm you. Perhaps add candles, crystals, prayer beads, or music.

★ _____
★ _____
★ _____
★ _____
★ _____
★ _____
★ _____
★ _____
★ _____
★ _____
★ _____
★ _____
★ _____
★ _____
★ _____
★ _____

Tiger

Power · Confidence · Dignity

Tigers represent physical prowess, courage, and inner strength. Native to Asia, the tiger has six current subspecies—the Sumatran tiger (the smallest of species), Siberian tiger, Bengal tiger, Indochinese tiger, South China tiger, and Malayan tiger. These majestic felines feature prominently in Asian philosophy and cosmology where their beauty and outer calm were thought to conceal their hidden ferocity. Through this balance of opposites, tigers embody harmony and the opposing forces of the Taoist yin and yang. In spirit form, tiger stripes and images were used on clothing or hung in the home as symbols of protection.

Unless mating or raising young, tigers are solitary and extremely territorial. Within their ideal range of 23 to 39 square miles, a tiger may have a number of dens in caves, hollow trees, and dense vegetation where they can hide. Powerful sprinters, swimmers, and climbers, tigers are incredible athletes. Sadly, their skills and prowess have been exploited in circuses and other animal shows. Thankfully, these cruel practices have now been banned across most of the world. These kings and queens of the jungle belong in the wild. If the tiger appears, they are calling you to explore the seemingly opposing forces of ferocity and calm inside you, and to find your innate strength by balancing them.

"If the tiger appears, they are calling you to explore the seemingly opposing forces of ferocity and calm inside you, and to find your innate strength by balancing them."

Ways to Connect with Tigers

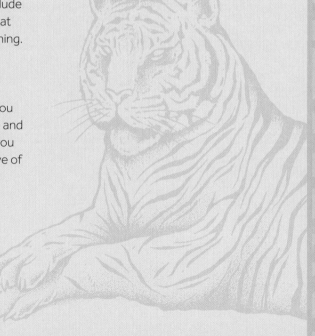

MEDITATION

Explore the innate strength and the balance of opposites within you. Call on the quiet strength of the tiger when you feel afraid.

SPECIES STATUS

The tiger has been listed as Endangered on the IUCN Red List of Threatened Species since 1986. Since the early 20th century, tiger populations have lost 93 percent of their historic range. Major reasons for population decline include habitat destruction, habitat fragmentation, and poaching.

NATURE CONNECTION

Explore the land around you with the quiet confidence and awareness of a tiger. Do you feel territorial or protective of this land?

ACTION

Engage with the various organizations listed at the back of this book that are helping to restore tiger habitats.

MOVEMENT

Take up a new sport to keep your body powerful, like that of a tiger. Try jogging, swimming, cycling, or a team sport.

Use this space to practice drawing a tiger. When you feel ready, grab a piece of paper or canvas and draw or paint a tiger. Hang this somewhere in your home where you'd like protection.

Connect with your intuition, dive into the depths of the ocean, and flow through rivers, emotions, and dreams with water-dwelling creatures like the humpback whale, dolphin, and sea otter.

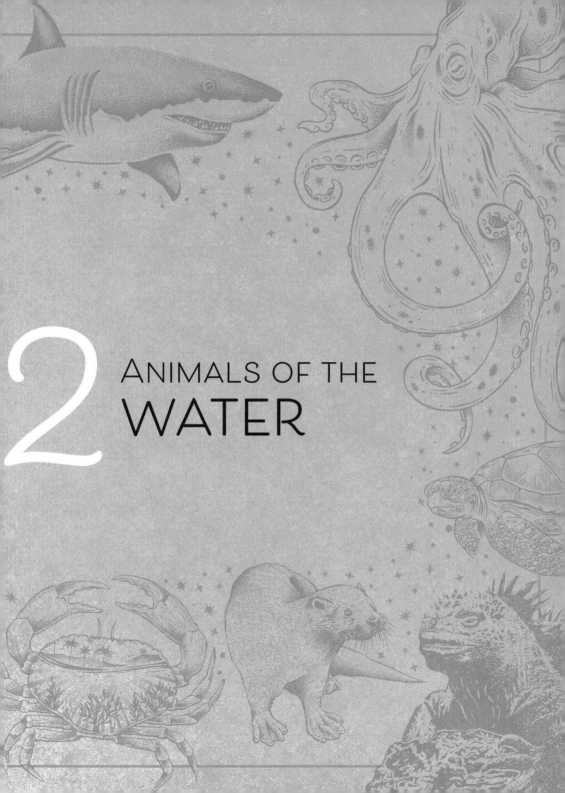

2 ANIMALS OF THE WATER

GREAT WHITE SHARK

Relentlessness · Hunger · Focus

Great white sharks play a vital role in ocean ecosystems. As apex predators, they ensure species diversity and keep their prey on the move, which indirectly maintains the health of important seagrass and coral reef habitats. Great whites are known to take extremely deep dives to feed on slow-moving fish and squid in the dark, cold waters of the sea. Though almost all fish are cold-blooded, these sharks have a specialized blood vessel structure that maintains a higher body temperature than the surrounding water. This allows them to move quickly and purposefully.

The great white shark asks us to confront and unmask our fears. While they are one of the few species known to have bitten and killed people, these events are extremely rare. People, on the other hand, capture too many great whites and scientists now consider them to be vulnerable to extinction. With fewer sharks in the coral reef ecosystem, larger predatory fish increase in abundance and feed on the herbivores. With fewer herbivores, macroalgae expand and coral can no longer compete, which threatens the survival of the reef system. If the shark has come up for you, it is time to dive into your own depths and ask: What am I truly hungry for? The shark asks you to dive inward, beyond any distractions or perceived threats, to find the true cravings of your soul.

"If the shark has come up for you, it is time to dive into your own depths and ask: What am I truly hungry for?"

Ways to Connect with Sharks

ACTIVITY

Get rid of unnecessary and excess stuff. Donate clothes and books, and recycle anything that you no longer use. Clear your space to increase your focus and clarity.

AWARENESS

Be an educated consumer and if you or your family eat seafood, be sure it comes from a sustainable source.

SPECIES STATUS

Due largely to overfishing, sharks are one of the most threatened groups of vertebrates on the planet. Great white sharks are now listed as Vulnerable on the IUCN Red List of Threatened Species. Throughout much of their range, they have been given some or complete legal protection, but bycatch and illegal poaching continue to occur.

ACTION

It is hard to get people to want to protect sharks when they are terrified by portrayals in the media like the movie *Jaws*. Help people to understand this misunderstood species. Do whatever you can to raise awareness on behalf of sharks, and share their important role in the ecosystem.

CREATIVE EXPLORATION

Set a timer for 10 minutes or more and write down all the things you crave. Remember, this is only for you, so don't edit—you can always destroy the list later. You might want to use the prompts "I am hungry for" or "I am starved for." Write non-stop until all your desires have spilled out from within. Let them do so without judgment until you arrive at the thing that has truly been gnawing at you, waiting to emerge.

SEAL

Balance · Longing · Inner Voice

Seals spend most of their lives in the sea, but they give birth on land. Rather than having external ears, seals have small openings, which shows their affinity with the inner voice. Seals swim both below and above water, giving them the ability to experience both the inner and outer worlds. The seal helps us to remember our connection to our deep personal rhythms and inner knowing.

In Celtic lore, these creatures are famous in the legends of the Selkies, seal people who can transform into humans by shedding their skin. These stories usually speak of an unassuming Selkie whose transformation is hampered by someone stealing her seal skin, forcing her to come onto land while she longs for the sea. In most tales about the Selkie woman, she eventually finds her skin, and after a life of love on land, she says goodbye and returns to the ocean. This reminds us that no one can steal our true identity—it is never lost, even if we slip away for a time. When we are not connected to our deepest self, we will always feel a sense of longing, but our "seal skin" is always there, ready and waiting to be reclaimed. If the seal enters your life, you are being called to dive within to reconnect with your soul, to retrieve your seal-skin and your true sense of purpose. The seal reminds us that we need the balance of both our inner and outer worlds in order to thrive.

"If the seal enters your life, you are being called to dive within to reconnect to your soul, to retrieve your seal-skin and your true sense of purpose."

Ways to Connect with Seals

NATURE CONNECTION

The seal is connected to both land and water. Find a place near you where the two meet and spend some time there.

SPECIES STATUS

While there are multiple protections in place to protect endangered seal species, their numbers are still struggling. Rapid ice loss in the Arctic causes seal pups to be separated from their mothers during the milking period, leading to high pup mortality. The Hawaiian monk seal faces threats like entanglement with fishing gear and food availability. Like other marine animals, seals need trash-free environments to help keep them from becoming extinct.

AWARENESS & ACTIVITY

Become informed about climate change and the impact on seals and other marine mammals, especially those who live in the Arctic. Can you get involved in activities that help them thrive? Perhaps you could pick up litter when hiking or on the beach.

MEDITATION

With the help of the seal, visualize diving inward to retrieve your deepest longings. You may not find your seal skin right away, but don't fret—you will find it one day. Set the intention to write and meditate for a number of days or weeks until your inner voice is clearly heard.

CREATIVE EXPLORATION

Write your own version of the Selkie story with yourself as the protagonist. What did you lose? How did that happen? How will you find the precious item again?

Octopus

Mystery · Intuition · Ingenuity

The octopus is a highly intelligent invertebrate found in every ocean of the world. Each of their eight arms is able to taste, touch, and move independently while their centralized brain exerts overall control. Amazingly, their arms can explore and solve problems while the rest of the octopus is busy doing something else. They can change shape and color, and blend in with their surroundings at will. They are even known to build little dens, using stones, shells, or even bits of broken glass to protect the entrance. The mimic octopus can contort their bodies and modify behavior to shapeshift into a wide variety of venomous animals to distract predators. Octopus ink can cause a blinding irritation for enemies while temporarily muddling their sense of smell and taste. With their liquid-like form, they are masters of escape and can slip in and out of incredibly tight spaces.

The octopus inspires us to let go of rigidity, be more flexible, and to tap into our own ability to sense our way through the world. They are agile, quick-thinking creatures who are gifted at abstract reasoning. Like the octopus, we can also understand our world through touch and sensation, and have the capacity to blend in and mimic our surroundings when necessary. If the octopus has slid into your life, it is time to loosen up, tap into your creativity, and think (with all of your senses) outside of the box.

"If the octopus has slid into your life, it is time to loosen up, tap into your creativity, and think (with all of your senses) outside of the box."

Ways to Connect with Octopuses

Activity

Wear something new, have fun taking on new shapes and forms, and find a new angle from which to deal with a challenge.

Species Status

Octopus are spread throughout large oceans and are solitary, which makes it difficult to determine the status of their populations. While their populations are not believed to be under threat, increasing noise pollution in the oceans from offshore drilling to ship motors and sonar use is putting them at risk. They are also impacted by the buildup of pollutants from land in their food chain—a process known as bioaccumulation. They consume prey that has retained toxins, which have an amplified impact as those toxins move up the food chain.

Movement

Is there a part of your body, a belief system, or habit that has become tense and rigid? Perhaps you spend too much time looking at screens? If so, stretch your body, examine your belief system, and begin to replace a monotonous habit with a more inspiring one.

Action

Help the octopus and other marine life by reducing pollution in the oceans. Be sure to use phosphate-free and environmentally friendly cleaners, detergents, and soaps, and encourage those around you to explore alternatives to chemical fertilizers that lead to the buildup of nutrients in the ocean, harming the creatures living there.

MEDITATION

Find a quiet and safe place, and then set a timer for at least 10 minutes. When you're ready, close your eyes and invite the octopus to meditate with you. Imagine yourself diving into their world: What will you find? What will they teach you? Journal or draw what you discovered.

CRAB

Rhythm · Protection · Sensitivity

Crabs live in fresh water, on land, and in all the world's oceans. These adaptable creatures are the symbol for the astrological water sign of Cancer, the fourth sign of the zodiac whose ruling planet is the Moon. Cancer is known for being an emotional, highly sensitive, and intuitive sign. A crab's hard shell offers protection against would-be predators, and is symbolic of self-preservation. They have a strong lunar connection and shed their hard exoskeletons in alignment with the Moon's cycle, spending a short time in a vulnerable soft-shell phase until they grow a new exterior as the Moon wanes and waxes again. In both phases, they burrow into the sandy ground for safety, symbolizing the need to know when to retreat for our own introspective seclusion.

The crab family displays massive variation between species—pea crabs are just a few millimeters wide, while the famous Japanese spider crab grows legs over 12 feet in length. These fascinating creatures can communicate by drumming or waving their pincers, and they usually walk sideways because of the articulation of their legs, reminding us that not all paths are straight and narrow. If the crab has crawled into your life, it is time to step back and take stock of your emotional wellbeing. Is it time to come out of your protective shell so you can grow?

"If the crab has crawled into your life, it is time to step back and take stock of your emotional wellbeing. Is it time to come out of your protective shell so you can grow?"

Ways to Connect with Crabs

SPECIES STATUS

The recent IUCN Red List assessment shows that about one-sixth of all freshwater crab species have an elevated risk of extinction, and only one-third are not at risk. The majority of threatened species are living in habitats subjected to deforestation, alteration of drainage patterns, and pollution.

ACTION

Become a water protector, and do what you can to prevent deforestation and pollution in your local area. Everything has a ripple effect. Act as another layer of protection for the crab and the habitats that they depend upon.

CREATIVE EXPLORATION

Try a sideways approach to a problem you are facing. Take time to withdraw and look at it from different angles and perspectives before approaching and tackling it again. For example, could you approach the problem using your senses? Or could you work backward from your goal? Thinking "outside of the box" is called lateral thinking. Use this space to document your findings until you come to a solution.

Nature Connection

Reflect on the cycles of the crab and attune to, and keep track of, the Moon's cycles. Do you feel any emotional or energetic shifts as the Moon waxes and wanes? Use this space to write about how you feel around the times of the New and Full Moon.

PLATYPUS

Unique · Unpredictable · Enigmatic

The platypus is one of the most unusual creatures in the animal kingdom, and one of just two mammals that lays eggs instead of giving birth to live young. Platypuses make their homes in freshwater areas that flow throughout the island of Tasmania and the eastern and southeastern coasts of Australia.

Platypuses hunt underwater, where they swim by paddling with their front webbed feet and steering with their hind feet and beaver-like tail. They have waterproof fur, skin that covers their eyes and ears, and noses that seal shut to protect the animals while they are underwater. Since they don't see or hear underwater, they find prey through electrolocation, using sensors on their bills that give them a sixth sense to detect tiny electrical fields. When platypuses find something interesting, like shellfish, insects, larvae, or worms, they scoop it up in their bills, store it in their cheek pouches, and swim to the surface. Since they only have grinding plates and no teeth, platypuses use any gravel they scooped up while on the bottom of the waterbed to mash their food into digestible pieces.

Platypuses usually spend their time hunting for food, and a hunt can last 10 to 12 hours. They are most active at night-time and dusk, and sleep during the day. When not hunting, they stay in their burrows. On land, the webbing on their feet retracts to expose individual nails and allows the creatures to run. Platypuses use their nails and feet to construct dirt burrows at the water's edge. The male platypus is one of the few species of venomous mammals, with a spur on his hind foot that delivers venom capable of causing severe pain. The unusual appearance of these egg-laying, duck-billed, beaver-tailed, otter-footed mammals baffled European naturalists when they first encountered them, and the first scientists to examine a platypus thought they were several animals sewn together.

While they might be unusual, the platypus reminds us to be ourselves no matter what others think. When the platypus comes into your life, it is time to learn to love yourself for who you are, especially your strangeness and perceived imperfections.

"When the platypus comes into your life, it is time to learn to love yourself for who you are, especially your strangeness and perceived imperfections."

Ways to Connect with Platypuses

MEDITATION

Can you sense or feel electricity? If we are tuned in to all the things around us, we feel them first before seeing them. Walk through your environment using subtle sensations and intuition to help you navigate.

SPECIES STATUS

Platypus numbers are declining, and in 2016 they were classified as Near Threatened in the IUCN Red List of Threatened Species. This is mainly due to urban and agricultural development, which causes habitat loss and population fragmentation. The platypus is also vulnerable to litter and the effects of pollution.

ACTION

On behalf of the platypus and animals in your area, challenge yourself and those around you to adopt zero-waste lifestyles. Recycle and reuse whenever possible and do your best to eat food that comes from local sources.

INNER EXPLORATION

What makes you unlike anyone or anything else? Do you try to hide your uniqueness or, like the platypus, do you embrace and celebrate it? Everyone has something that makes them special. Look in the mirror and deep within to list everything that makes you unique.

MARINE IGUANA

Adaptability • Meditative Stillness • Depth

Marine iguanas are the world's only ocean-going lizard and live exclusively on the Galapagos Islands off the coast of Ecuador. It is thought that marine iguanas rafted over water from South America 10–15 million years ago.

Marine iguanas nest on rocky ledges and dive to the bottom of the ocean for nourishment. Excellent swimmers, they move easily through the water as they feed on algae. They can dive as deep as 66 feet and can spend up to one hour foraging underwater. In the mornings, they bask in the sun to absorb heat until they have energy to swim out again.

These unique animals are associated with depth, stoicism, and meditative stillness. Adults shed their skin in pieces to completely renew once a year, reminding us to let go of what we've outgrown. They have a third eye located on the top of their head called a parietal eye that perceives various shades of light and different shapes for heightened awareness. When under tremendous shock or threat, the iguana plays dead and waits for the situation to pass, reminding us that sometimes the best thing to do in a difficult situation is surrender. If this unique creature has shown up for you, it is an invitation to dive inward to the fascinating, never-ending depths of your imagination.

"If this unique creature has shown up for you, it is an invitation to dive inward to the fascinating, never-ending depths of your imagination."

Ways to Connect with Marine Iguanas

NATURE CONNECTION

Spend time near the ocean or an expanse of fresh water and learn about the wild algae or seaweed nearby. Sit or lie in the sun in a state of meditative stillness.

SPECIES STATUS

Classified as Vulnerable on the IUCN Red List of Threatened Species. El Niño periodically decreases the iguana population (by up to 85 percent), as it cuts short their food supplies. Oil spills have similarly dramatic effects on the population in addition to the introduction of non-native predators like cats and dogs, and plastic pollution—specifically microplastics.

INNER EXPLORATION

What do I need to shed? Is there a situation I need to surrender to? What answers lie underneath the realm of my conscious awareness? Do I need time to simply be?

DREAMWORK

Water relates to the emotional and dream realms. Ask a question before you go to sleep at night and invite the iguana to dive into the subconscious depths and return to the surface with answers. Write down or draw anything you remember or feel when you wake up.

Dolphin

Communication · Cooperation · Compassion

Dolphins are intensely social mammals that communicate with squeaks, whistles, and clicks. They can be found in every ocean, and some, like Amazon River dolphins, live in fresh water. They track their prey using echolocation with their signature clicks which bounce sound waves off nearby creatures, revealing their location, size, and shape. Dolphins are fast and graceful swimmers, famous for their playful personalities. They live and travel in groups called pods that may combine for several minutes or hours to form larger social groups called herds. In deep parts of the ocean there have been reports of communities reaching over a mile in length.

Every dolphin develops a specific whistle called a signature whistle that functions like their name. Studies have shown that dolphins can remember the signature whistles of companions or rivals for up to 20 years. Known for their altruistic tendencies, dolphins may come to the aid of injured dolphins, using their unique call to summon help, and if needed, provide physical support for the weakened animal by bringing them to the surface to breathe. There are also stories of bottlenose dolphins saving humans from shark attacks and directing stranded whales back out to the open sea. If the dolphin appears, they may be calling you to help those in need while harnessing the strength and power of community.

"If the dolphin appears, they may be calling you to help those in need while harnessing the strength and power of community."

Ways to Connect with Dolphins

CREATIVE EXPLORATION

Do you have a preferred way of communicating, like the dolphin? Do you prefer verbal, non-verbal, written, or even visual communication? If you're always texting friends and family, why not try calling, or sending a letter?

SPECIES STATUS

While their populations remain healthy, current threats to dolphins come from being caught accidentally in commercial fishing nets, warming ocean temperatures, and noise pollution. Dolphins must rise regularly to the surface to breathe— becoming entangled in nets prevents this, leading to drowning. Warming ocean temperatures due to climate change have caused primary food sources to move into deeper, cooler water, while increasing noise pollution in the oceans has a significant impact on dolphins and whales since they depend on acoustics for survival.

ACTION

Gather a group of friends or family to work on behalf of a conservation cause you care about. There is strength in numbers.

MEDITATION

Meditate with the dolphin as your guide, as you imagine swimming in and out of dolphin pods. What does it feel like to move with such ease in and out of different communities? Write about or draw your experience.

SEAHORSE

Awareness · Partnership · Patience

With keen awareness, the seahorse moves slowly from place to place using only their tails as anchors in stormy seas. These patient and persistent creatures are named for the mythological Hippocampus, a half horse, half fish found in Greek and Roman mythology. A mythological seahorse also appears in Pictish stone carvings in Scotland where they are known as Kelpies—shapeshifting water spirits.

Seahorses are small syngnathid fishes—the only animal family in which the males, not the females, carry the young. Seahorses mate for life and the male carries the female's eggs for about one and a half months in a tail pouch until fully formed, miniature seahorses are eventually released. These creatures live in temperate salt water throughout the world in shallow seagrass beds, estuaries, coral reefs, and mangroves where they protect themselves by blending into their surroundings. They have eyes that can look in opposite directions at the same time, giving them the ability to see different perspectives simultaneously. It's interesting to note that the hippocampus in our body's limbic system is shaped like a seahorse and plays an important role in spatial navigation and memory storage. If the seahorse has shown up for you, they are calling you to look at challenges from every direction while finding new and exciting ways to support the ones you love.

> "*If the seahorse has shown up for you, they are calling you to look at challenges from every direction while finding new and exciting ways to support the ones you love.*"

Ways to Connect with Seahorses

NATURE CONNECTION

Walk in nature and take special note of the sights, smells, and shapes of plants or trees in places that move you. Make a mental note of them and use them as markers to navigate and remember your way back.

SPECIES STATUS

Coral reefs and seagrass beds are deteriorating, reducing viable habitats for seahorses. According to the IUCN Red List of Threatened Species, 12 species are Vulnerable and two are Endangered, but 17 other species are listed as data deficient. Learn more about the various challenges seahorses face and find ways to raise awareness and help this unique creature.

MEDITATION

Remember a place in nature—perhaps a local park, wood, or meadow—that you feel especially drawn and bonded to. Close your eyes and take yourself there as vividly as possible. Set a timer for at least 10 minutes and imagine yourself wandering throughout this special landscape.

ACTION

Offer to help others.
Do something you
wouldn't normally
do to lift the weight
off someone else's
shoulders—even
if this is just doing
some cooking
or cleaning—or
alleviate the stress
of someone you
love. Journal about
the experience here.

HUMPBACK WHALE

Consciousness · Mystery · Soul Song

Humpback whales have been traveling and singing throughout the world's oceans for millions of years. This ancient mammal is a symbol of incredible transformation and is believed to have evolved from terrestrial hoofed mammals some 45 million years ago. A species of baleen whale, humpbacks travel slowly and steadily to cover 16,000 miles in an average season. Their haunting calls, sung by male humpbacks, can go on for hours and carry for miles beneath the sea. Unlike humans who breathe involuntarily, these intelligent beings must be conscious of their breath. To go to sleep and still breathe, they shut off just half their brain at a time, which aligns them with conscious awareness and lucid dreaming.

If this gentle giant comes into your life, slow down and listen. You may be asked to dive deep within. Since water relates to the emotional realm, to dreams, and to the unconscious, perhaps there's something that is ready to emerge from the depths of your inner world. This whale reminds you to be conscious of your breath as you travel inward. These patient beings take their time but travel far. Is there a journey of the soul you're ready to begin?

"If this gentle giant comes into your life, slow down and listen. You may be asked to dive deep within."

Ways to Connect with Whales

Nature Connection
Go to the nearest ocean, lake, or river. Then meditate, walk, and sing next to the expanse of water. Allow sounds to come up from the depths of you.

Species Status
These gentle giants were once hunted to the brink of extinction. Killing humpback whales is now illegal, though risks for this species still exist.

Action
Pick up plastic and trash at the beach and encourage your friends to do the same. Human impact is a huge threat to these ancient beings. Consider reducing or eliminating plastic consumption—use cloth bags and avoid using plastic drinking straws.

ACTIVITIES

Create a whale song.
Listen to some examples
on YouTube and try to
copy the sounds.

Learn more about this
ancient species and jot
down what you find out.

DREAMWORK

Dreams awaken
what may be hidden
underneath the
realm of conscious
awareness, to help
us heal. Ask the
humpback to help
you navigate internal
waters and support
you in deep, dark
places while you
dream. Keep this
book by your bed and
write down anything
you remember or
feel when you wake.

MEDITATION

Play a humpback whale song while you meditate or simply sit and listen to the haunting melody. You could also attend a sound bath (a group experience where you are "bathed" in sound waves from instruments). Write about or draw what comes up for you. during this time.

TREE FROG

Song · New Beginnings · Transformation

Frogs undergo an incredible transformation from egg, to tadpole, to fully formed amphibian. The word amphibian is derived from a Greek word meaning "two lives" since frogs can live on both land and water. As tadpoles, they feed on algae, which helps filter water and keep it clean, and when they are fully grown, they feed on insects such as mosquitoes. Despite their name, not all tree frogs live in trees. The feature that unites them has to do with their feet—the last bone in their toes is shaped like a claw. Since their weight has to be carried by the branches and twigs of the plants and trees in their habitats, they are usually tiny and vary widely in color and patterns. Some species can assume the color of their surroundings to protect themselves from predators.

Though they are tiny, their voices are large and their chorus can envelop the forests and lands where they live. These amphibians are known by scientists as indicator species since they are among the first to be affected by environmental imbalances. They have very sensitive skin and pores, which they breathe through, and are dependent on the health of both the land and the water. If the tree frog comes into your life, it may be time to listen carefully to the small and sensitive aspects of yourself and to use your voice to make those parts of you heard.

"If the tree frog comes into your life, it may be time to listen carefully to the small and sensitive aspects of yourself and to use your voice to make those parts of you heard."

Ways to Connect with Frogs

Species Status

Despite living millions of years, frogs are now dying off in record numbers. Nearly one-third of amphibian species are threatened with extinction. Amphibians are declining worldwide and are collectively one of the most at-risk groups for extinction. Tree frogs are found on every continent except Antarctica. Threats to tree frogs include habitat destruction, pollution, and climate change. Now rescue centers and other institutions worldwide are working together on an "Amphibian Ark" to help save species as they vanish in the wild, in the hope of one day returning them home.

Inner Exploration

Are you sensitive to aspects of your environment? What are the strengths of your unique sensitivity? What important information is being shown to you that you might share with other people?

Action

Volunteer as a citizen scientist, joining a local group to research and restore local wetlands, and inform those around you of the plight of frogs and the dangers of pollutants such as pesticides. Research safe alternatives and share your findings with others.

MEDITATION

Set aside some time to sit outside and close your eyes. Use the power of your senses and sensitivity to explore the information coming to you from the outside world. Use stream-of-consciousness writing to explore what you can sense.

Sea Otter

Affection · Cooperation · Play

The sea otter is an adorable and charismatic marine mammal of the North Pacific Ocean, and one of the largest species in the weasel family. They are the only species in that family that live their entire lives in the ocean, preferring rocky shores and kelp forests. Sea otters like to float on their backs, going with the flow, and as they do, they often hold hands so they can stay connected. Holding hands keeps them together and also keeps their delicate paw pads warm. Since they also sleep on their backs on the surface of the water, they often wrap themselves in giant kelp to stop them floating away, which is a constant worry for these animals. Pups are born with such buoyant fur that they float like corks on top of the water and are completely dependent on their mother for the first six months of their lives.

These creatures are foragers that eat mostly hard-shelled invertebrates, including sea urchins and a variety of clams, mussels, and crabs. When they dive to collect invertebrates, they also retrieve a large rock to smash their shelled prey so they can get to the soft parts.

If the otter shows up for you, it is time to reflect on what is most precious to you. Is there anything in your life that is at risk of floating away? There is a delicate balance between clinging and caring. The sea otter reminds us to love, and at the same time, to go with the flow.

"If the otter shows up for you, it is time to reflect on what is most precious to you. Is there anything in your life that is at risk of floating away?"

Ways to Connect with Otters

SPECIES STATUS

In the 18th and 19th centuries, sea otter pelts were highly valued for making coats and other outerwear, and the species was nearly hunted to extinction. Scientists estimate the total population reached levels less than one percent of their pre-hunt numbers. Sea otters now have legal protection throughout much of their range, and there has been some recovery in recent decades. However, scientists still believe that populations are decreasing as a result of oil pollution, changes to food webs in the North Pacific, and habitat loss, and this species is considered Endangered (highly vulnerable to extinction) on the IUCN Red List. Without continuing conservation measures and legal protection, this charismatic species could be at risk of being lost forever.

NATURE CONNECTION

Life is a playground. We don't need toys, video games, or other contraptions to find joy. Go outside and find joy, but be sure not to disturb other creatures as you do so. Follow the lead of your otter ally, who is playful, but also considerate.

ACTION

Get involved in water protection of all kinds and tend to your local rivers or oceans by joining an organized conservation group that protects water and wetland habitats, so that otters (and other animals) have places to love, live, relax, and play.

Is something or someone you care for at risk of floating away? Explore this idea. What is most important for you to hold onto? Write a letter, make a call, or spend time with that person, animal, or place to strengthen your bonds. Use this space to paste special photos of that person, animal, or place. Or, if you enjoy drawing, why not make a sketch of them using a reference photo?

TURTLE

Mindfulness · Sagacity · Slowing Down

Turtles have long lifespans and are one of the most ancient reptile groups on Earth. One reason they are believed to live so long is their slowness, which prevents them from aging like we do as a result of our fast-paced lives. The longest-lived of all the turtle species is the Galapagos giant tortoise, a peace-loving creature with a heavy, cumbersome shell which can live to be over 100 years old.

Although many turtles spend a large proportion of their lives underwater, all turtles and tortoises breathe air. So turtles need to surface at regular intervals to refill their lungs. Because of their slow metabolisms, they can survive for long periods without food or water, giving them a greater chance of survival in harsh conditions. In stories like the "Tortoise and the Hare," the tortoise is a symbol of steady, calm wisdom, reminding us to slow down and think. When we rush around obsessed with being "first" like the hare, we are often wasting precious energy. If the turtle shows up for you, it is time to take stock of the way you are using your energy. Is it wise? Are you rushing around and wasting your time? The turtle asks us to reflect on the root of our motivations and move forward mindfully.

"If the turtle shows up for you, it is time to take stock of the way you are using your energy."

Ways to Connect with Turtles

NATURE CONNECTION

Take a day, or even a week, to move about the world slowly and look at the land around you from a turtle's point of view. Notice the details, the textures, the colors. Approach everything with calm intention. How does it feel to move slowly and mindfully, like a turtle? Do you experience resistance or restlessness? If so, journal about the feeling and explore why. If you enjoy this, begin to do it more often, even developing it into a regular practice.

SPECIES STATUS

Of the 360 known turtle species, many are critically endangered. Of the seven species of sea turtles that call the United States home, unfortunately six are listed as Vulnerable, Endangered, or Critically Endangered by the IUCN Red List of Threatened Species.

ACTION

Learn about the turtle species in your area. What challenges do they face? Get involved in their conservation and refuse to buy anything that is made with real tortoiseshell such as souvenirs and jewelry. This is threatening the beautiful hawksbill sea turtle with extinction.

CREATIVE EXPLORATION

Take some time to step back and slow down. Draw or write about all the things you "do," such as school, hobbies, and sports. Which ones matter the most to you? If you feel too busy, how can you find more calm, steadiness, and spaciousness?

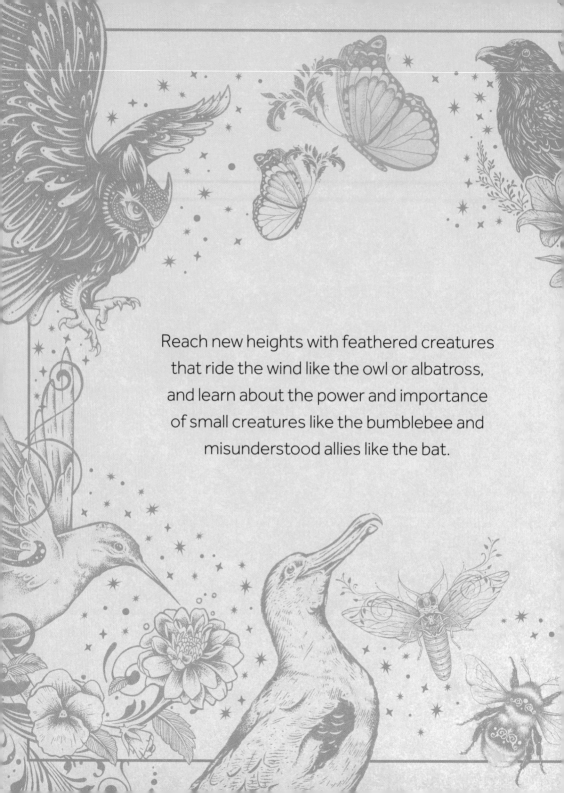

Reach new heights with feathered creatures
that ride the wind like the owl or albatross,
and learn about the power and importance
of small creatures like the bumblebee and
misunderstood allies like the bat.

3 ANIMALS OF THE AIR

BUTTERFLY

Change · Trust · Letting Go

The butterfly teaches us that true beauty and growth come with inevitable struggle. If this creature comes into your life, you might be on the cusp of profound personal change. Change is rarely easy, and no insect undergoes a more complete and total transformation than the butterfly. In the chrysalis stage, a caterpillar liquifies and lets go of their former self before they grow wings and become a butterfly. They must endure wrestling out of the cocoon, and in turn, build the strength to fly.

Once they emerge there are few creatures that can rival their beauty. However, their life is fleeting—reminding us that time and life are precious. We lose out when we stay safe in a cocoon. It's time for you to brave the inevitable struggle, so you appreciate the wonders of the world, open your wings, and fly.

Butterflies are important pollinators on every continent (except Antarctica) and are indicators of a healthy ecosystem. Many species migrate over long distances, which allows pollen to be shared across plant families that are far apart from one another. The term "butterfly effect" refers to their role in the web of life and the chain reaction that occurs in their presence or absence.

Tune in to reflect on the power of your own actions or inactions, to create a butterfly effect. Is it time to wrestle out of old belief systems?

"If this creature comes into your life, you might be on the cusp of profound personal change."

Ways to Connect with Butterflies

Species Status

There are many species of butterflies throughout the world. Many are categorized as Endangered on the IUCN Red List of Threatened Species.

Awareness

Learn more about how human activities are having a negative impact on the world's butterflies. The use of pesticides and the loss of natural habitats affect the food sources of these beautiful insects.

Meditation

We all go through periods of change and self-development. What massive change is taking place within you. Find a quiet space and reflect on the process of transformation and metamorphosis.

Nature Connection

Plant native wildflowers that are critical to butterflies. In the United States, for example, the monarch butterfly relies on milkweed, which is becoming endangered due to pesticide use. Do your research and help create more beauty in the world by planting flowers and providing habitats where these stunning creatures can fly.

CREATIVE EXPLORATION

Draw your own colorful butterfly wings here, as you contemplate your personal transformation. Where will they take you on your life's journey?

Owl

Navigation · Presence · Inner Knowing

The owl is a master at maneuvering through the shadows and can help us navigate unseen realms. The wise and watchful owl appears to us when transition is near. During medieval times, in Western and Central Europe, it was thought that priestesses and wizards could shapeshift into owls. The legendary Merlin from King Arthur's court is often pictured with an owl as his familiar or companion. In Buddhism, the owl is the enemy of ignorance, helping uncover knowledge that is hidden in darkness. In Greek mythology, the owl is sacred to Athena, the Greek goddess of learning.

These predatory birds have extremely large eyes which are fixed in front, unlike other bird species. As a result, they must rotate their heads to observe their surroundings, and can turn them a full 270 degrees. They rival cats for having the best night vision in the animal kingdom and have unique feathers that enable them to fly almost silently. They have extremely sensitive ears to pinpoint the exact location of their prey. Owls can often be found hunting in eerie, deserted places such as cemeteries. Instead of building their own nests, most owls will take over the abandoned nests of other birds and animals. They reside in barns, deserted buildings, or tree hollows. If the owl has shown up for you, then it may be time to face your inner and outer shadows.

> *"If the owl has shown up for you, then it may be time to face your inner and outer shadows."*

Ways to Connect with Owls

SPECIES STATUS

There are 134 known species of owls in the world. The Eurasian eagle owl is the largest and the elf owl is the smallest. Human impact and deforestation has led to the decline of many owl populations.

NATURE CONNECTION

Sit outside in the dark with a friend or family member and allow your senses to adjust. Learn the call of owls that live near you. Perhaps use your cellphone to record their calls. If you live in an urban area, you can still learn about the owls that live nearby. Be mindful that owls are easily startled by humans and may abandon their nests and young if you get too close or make too much noise.

ACTION

Some species of owls are declining due to habitat loss, so conservationists encourage people to create nesting and roosting structures. Build an owl house in a nearby wood or wild area. Owl houses are especially popular with barn owls.

MEDITATION

Meditate in darkness and ask the question: What inner wisdom is ready to be revealed to me? Invite the owl to be your guide and write down all that you find out together.

EAGLE

Confidence · Intensity · Perspective

Eagles are the top predators in the avian world. With keen eyesight, these large birds can see four times farther than humans and can detect the movement of their prey two miles away. They can fly up to 35 miles per hour and reach speeds of over 100 miles per hour or more when diving and hunting. These confident birds build their nests in tall trees or on high cliffs where they can see far and wide, with big-picture vision, while narrowing in on the details.

Some eagles migrate while others remain in their ranges throughout their lives. If all goes well, eagles can live between 35–40 years in the wild. They hunt during the day, usually from a high perch, and feed by swooping over open water or land and catching their meals with sharply curved talons. The female of all known species of eagle is larger than the male.

There are eagles all over the world; most live in Europe, Asia, and Africa with just two species found in North America and more in Central and South America and Australia. Although the bald eagle is the most famous in the United States as the country's emblem, the most powerful eagle in the region is the golden eagle. The golden eagle is America's largest bird of prey and also the national bird of Mexico. These beautiful birds are also found in Asia, northern Africa, and Europe. Golden eagle pairs maintain territories that may be as large as 60 square miles. They are monogamous and may remain with their mate for several years or possibly for life.

For many decades, eagles around the world were hunted for sport and for the misguided protection of livestock and fishing grounds. Now, with increased protections, these magnificent birds are making a comeback in the wild.

With the support of the eagle, we can look far into the future, seeing what's ahead, while remaining focused on our goals. In pursuit, the eagle's keen awareness helps us maneuver around obstacles that may be in our way. When the eagle soars in your life, it is time to rise above the details and shift your awareness to long-term vision and a big-picture perspective.

"*When the eagle soars in your life, it is time to rise above the details and shift your awareness to long-term vision and a big-picture perspective.*"

Ways to Connect with Eagles

MEDITATION

Imagine soaring over a problem or over your life as a whole. Zoom out. What do you see? What stands out and comes into focus as being important? How has your perspective shifted? Take some time to journal about what you find.

SPECIES STATUS

Human-sourced threats include habitat change, persecution, poisoning (often directed at other species), collisions with man-made objects, and human population growth, which have made areas historically used by eagles unsuitable, both in terms of habitat and prey availability. While many eagles around the world are making a comeback due to increased protections, species like the Beaudouin's snake eagle and the Kinabalu serpent eagle are listed as Vulnerable on the IUCN Red List of Threatened Species, while the Madagascar serpent eagle is listed as Endangered.

NATURE CONNECTION

Hike to the top of a hill or climb a tree with a friend to gain the perspective of an eagle. Look far and wide. Take some deep breaths and get distance from the details of everyday life. Viewing a difficult situation or problem from afar can help put things into perspective.

ACTION

Encourage those around you to retain tall trees, especially around water, as perch and nesting sites. Eagles love old, tall, and dead trees where they can perch and see without obstruction. Protect wintering and nesting areas, and leave them undisturbed. Human contact with these areas can make eagles abandon them.

CREATIVE EXPLORATION

Draw a challenge in your life from eagle's point of view. What does the landscape or situation look like from above? Is there anything that needs to be rearranged in order to manifest your vision of the future? If so, draw another map that represents the future you want to create.

HUMMINGBIRD

Joy · Radiance · Remembrance

A group of hummingbirds can be called a bouquet, a glittering, or a shimmer, and with their iridescent feathers and sparkling colors, hummingbirds look like flying gems. They can fly forward, backward, and even upside down, and their brain is larger in comparison to body size than any other bird species. These smart pollinators have an enlarged hippocampus, the brain region responsible for spatial memory, which they use to remember every flower in their territory, which is vast, and essential for survival. Their high metabolism makes them vulnerable to starvation, and species like the ruby-throated hummingbird burn energy so quickly, they must consume more than their own weight in nectar and insects every day to stay alive. As such, these small, mostly solitary birds are very territorial. In adverse conditions when no food can be found, hummingbirds can enter a state called torpor, similar to what we term hibernation in mammals, in which their metabolism slows down tremendously.

These gorgeous creatures will play in shallow bird baths, fly through misting water, or rub themselves against wet leaves after rain. If the hummingbird comes into your life, then it is time to embrace and celebrate the joy and beauty of the natural world—dance in the rain and soak in the light of the Sun.

"If the hummingbird comes into your life, then it is time to embrace and celebrate the joy and beauty of the natural world—dance in the rain and soak in the light of the Sun."

Ways to Connect with Hummingbirds

SPECIES STATUS

Despite the fact that hummingbirds are found only in North, South, and Central America, and islands of the Caribbean, they are known across the globe. Hummingbirds are the world's second-largest family of birds with an estimated 338 species, and now nearly ten percent of these species are threatened with extinction, according to an analysis by BirdLife International.

ACTION

Create more beauty in your backyard. If there are hummingbirds in your area, instead of putting out sugar water, learn which flowers they prefer and plant a mix of native flower species like salvia, honeysuckle, monarda, and mallow to provide natural food. If you do put out sugar water, do not use food coloring, as many do, as this is toxic to birds. You will bring joy to all who see the hummingbirds and will also be helping bees and butterflies.

NATURE CONNECTION

Look at the world from the point of view of a hummingbird and navigate your way on a walk using flowers or other markers of natural beauty—perhaps a small stream, a beautiful tree, a misting rain.

CREATIVE EXPLORATION

Bring more joy and sweetness into your life. Make a list of all the activities, people, and experiences that fill you with happiness. Keep the list private and engage in at least one thing on your list each day.

FIREFLY

Inner Spark · Magic · Wonder

Fireflies are beetles whose magical light displays capture our imagination. The flashes of light we see are the firefly language of love. Male fireflies flash a specific pattern while they fly, hoping a female will reply. If a female waiting in the grass or bushes likes what she sees, she will respond with a flash of her own. There are more than 2,000 species of fireflies found all over the world, on every continent except Antarctica, and each species has its own light language and pattern. These insects are incredibly diverse, and there can be many species sharing one habitat. It is likely that there are a variety of species flashing around us in the warm, summer months. While the twinkling lights of fireflies are seen as an expression of summer in the temperate regions, there is one North American species that is active in the winter. Adults of these winter fireflies do not emit light; instead, they hide in the bark of trees and largely go unnoticed.

This enchanting insect is symbolic of our inner light, and offers the medicine of being seen. It reminds us to make peace with darkness, for it is only in darkness that we can see the stars. When the firefly illuminates your life, it is time to shine.

"When the firefly illuminates your life, it is time to shine."

Ways to Connect with Fireflies

NATURE CONNECTION

If there are fireflies active in your area now, pay close attention to their unique blinks and try to identify the language of the different species.

SPECIES STATUS

Like most insects, fireflies are threatened by the use of pesticides and light pollution. The Center for Biological Diversity is working to ensure that at-risk fireflies, such as the Bethany Beach firefly, get the protection they need to prevent extinction.

ACTION

Do whatever you can to eliminate the use of harmful pesticides—write letters to your local town representatives and try to buy organic products—and let yourself be driven by what you care for, allowing yourself to be heard and seen.

MEDITATION

Set a timer and spend 10 minutes or more in darkness to find your inner spark. Once you do, breathe into and imagine your inner light expanding. Do your best to sit through any restlessness or inner discomfort. When the timer goes off, write about what you found and how it makes you shine in the world.

BUMBLEBEE

Sweetness · Attraction · Devotion

Bumblebees spend their lives creating sweetness and beauty. One out of every three bites of food we eat depends on pollinators, and bumblebees are especially important. These adorable fuzzy insects have small, somewhat disorderly nests with 50 to 500 bees. Unlike honey bees, bumblebees only exist in the wild and usually build their hives close to the ground under fallen leaves, piles of wood, in abandoned mouse holes, or beneath compost. After busy seasons of pollination, the entire colony dies off, except for the queen. She hibernates over winter before starting a new colony in spring. This is why it's important to leave areas of yards, parks, and other outdoor spaces a little wild. If just one queen dies, an entire potential colony is lost.

Only the female worker bees go out to collect nectar and pollen while the males clean and guard the nest and eventually go out looking to start colonies with new queens. It is also only the female bumblebee that has stingers, and she will only sting if truly provoked. They are even known to warn before stinging by sticking up a middle leg, telling you to "Back Off." But they are so gentle that they will only sting if they feel threatened or incredibly annoyed. After all, they have important work to do. Bumblebees can sting more than once; their stinger lacks barbs and so is not left behind when they sting. Since their work requires a lot of energy, a bumblebee might rest in or around flowers. So if you see a bee that isn't moving, it doesn't mean she is dead. She might just be taking a nap!

Bumblebees make small amounts of honey, just enough to tide them over a few days of bad weather, so they need to forage regularly to survive. Now they have to work harder than ever to find food and shelter due to habitat loss and the overuse of pesticides. We can help bumblebees by rewilding land and creating more beauty. If the bumblebee buzzes into your life, you are being called to plant flowers, tend to the small but important spaces within, and to cultivate your own natural beauty.

"*If the bumblebee buzzes into your life, you are being called to plant flowers, tend to the small but important spaces within, and to cultivate your own natural beauty.*"

Ways to Connect with Bumblebees

Action

To attract bumblebees and other native bee species, consider planting native plants and perennials, and do not use pesticides. Since bumblebees are able to fly in cooler temperatures and lower light conditions than other bees, plan your garden to have a long season of bloom. Many plants like clover, goldenrod, dandelion, and thistle that humans consider to be weeds provide important food for bumblebees. Help change the perception of these flowers so that bumblebees can thrive. Provide nesting sites by leaving some part of your yard a little wild. Don't mow or rake there to give the new queen a place to hibernate and establish a new colony in spring.

Species Status

There are over 255 species of bumblebees found all over the world, but many are listed as Endangered, Vulnerable, or Near Threatened on the IUCN Red List of Threatened Species. The rusty patched bumblebee became the first wild bee to receive federal protection in the United States under the Endangered Species Act.

ACTIVITY

Use this space to take note of all the flowers growing around you, whether in your backyard or local park. Then learn to identify them. What is blooming, and where? What species are they? Set the intention that when the time is right, you will plant more wildflowers in these spaces and encourage your neighbors to do so as well.

RAVEN

Mystery · Confidence · Esoteric Wisdom

The raven is a messenger of mystery and esoteric wisdom. These ubiquitous birds have coexisted with humans for thousands of years. Their ingenuity, adaptability, and versatile diet have helped them succeed as a species. They are bold, playful, and walk with a confident swagger on the ground. In flight, ravens can tumble, roll, fly upside down, and dive to catch objects in midair. In many myths, ravens have reputations for being wise tricksters who are terrible at keeping secrets.

In Native American Mythology, Raven brought light and fire to the world, and Kutkh is a similar raven spirit in the cosmology of the indigenous peoples of Russia. Kutkh brought light, water, language, and crafts, but as the trickster, can also be a thief. Raven symbolism is associated with the Welsh hero Bran, the Blessed, the holder of ancestral memories and wisdom, whose name means raven. The Norse god Odin was accompanied by two ravens that soared across the lands each day and returned to tell him of all they had seen. When the raven flies into your life it is time to embrace mystery, and journey bravely into the unknown. The raven is the messenger of intrigue.

"When the raven flies into your life it is time to embrace mystery, and journey bravely into the unknown."

Ways to Connect with Ravens

SPECIES STATUS

There are species of raven throughout the world. Their populations are healthy and, in fact, seem to be increasing.

MEDITATION

Try a special meditation that enables you to move through space and time. Simply close your eyes and visualize a raven companion. Send them flying into your past, and then into your future, and then allow them to come back into the present. What wisdom or important pieces of information have they found and brought back to you?

NATURE CONNECTION

Learn to distinguish ravens from crows. With practice, crows and ravens can be distinguished by the calls they make. Listen carefully. The call of a raven is often described as a deep, hollow croak, while the crow call is described as a caw. Their tails are also shaped differently, and the raven has a much more prominent beak and is about twice the size of the crow!

CREATIVE EXPLORATION

Choose one of the ancient myths about the raven described on page 166, then use the myth for inspiration to write a poem or short story.

ALBATROSS

Endurance · Loyalty · Partnership

Albatrosses are seabirds capable of traveling 10,000 miles in a single journey. They rely on the wind to help them soar over vast oceans for hours without rest and have the longest wingspan of any bird, reaching up to 11 and a half feet. They can fly up to 50 miles per hour, and can circle the globe in just 46 days. These birds are rarely seen on land and gather only to breed, at which time they form large colonies on remote islands.

Albatross fidelity is legendary, and like us, they take time to pick a partner. In order to find the right mate, they perform elaborate song and dance rituals that include clicks, screams, and graceful wing positioning. At first, these dances happen in small groups, until gradually the numbers whittle down and each bird dances with only one. When they find their mate, they snuggle and preen each other tenderly and most do not find another, even if their partner dies. Mating pairs produce a single egg that they take turns caring for. Albatrosses can live for up to 50 years and beyond.

These amazing birds overcome incredible odds to find and reunite with their partners, showing us that love can stay strong even when we're apart. If the albatross soars into your life, it is a message to reflect upon who and what you are most committed to and tend to those relationships for stronger and healthier bonds.

"If the albatross soars into your life, it is a message to reflect upon who and what you are most committed to and tend to those relationships for stronger and healthier bonds."

Ways to Connect with Albatrosses

SPECIES STATUS

The albatross has existed for about 50 million years, but now all 22 species are among the world's most endangered birds. Eight are Critically Endangered, nine are classed as Vulnerable, and the remaining five are likely to become Endangered, according to the IUCN Red List of Threatened Species. Fishing and plastic are big problems. Since albatrosses can only plunge into the top few feet of the ocean to look for squid and fish eggs, they often encounter plastic floating on the surface. The Laysan albatross is particularly attracted to this debris and eats the plastic, mistaking it for food. They then fly back to the nest and feed bottle caps, buttons, and other waste to their young who often starve to death because their stomachs are full of plastic.

MEDITATION

Explore the currents of energy in your life. Are you going with the flow? If so, is it bringing you to your desired destination? Perhaps you want to establish a meditation practice or eat more mindfully but can't break old habits. If you are struggling to reach a new goal, can you cut across the currents, change your approach, and follow a different path to help you get there?

ACTION

Most marine pollution is litter that starts out on land. You can help the albatross by recycling, and choosing reusable alternatives over single-use plastic. Less plastic on land means less plastic in the ocean!

Nature Connection

Take a day, a week, or even a month to attune to the wind. Notice and learn about the directions of the breeze. Is it coming from the north, south, east, or west? Where would the breeze take you if you could soar like the albatross and go wherever you wished? Write about your journey.

BAT

Acute Perception · Initiation · Rebirth

Bats are aligned with the liminal times of dusk and dawn, when day becomes night and night becomes day. If the bat has come up for you, it may be time to embrace the healing power of darkness and awaken the amazing power of your senses. These mysterious mammals sleep upside down in trees, rock crevices, caves, and buildings during the day and wake at dusk to begin their work. Using sound, bats can see everything but color and can detect the mosquitoes they prey on and objects as imperceptible as spider webs without light. Some species can catch up to 600 mosquitoes in an hour. And while many bats are insectivores, others are fruit-eaters, which provides us with sweetness because they are important pollinators for plants such as mango, banana, and agave. Many tropical plants depend entirely on bats to pollinate their flowers and disperse the seeds.

For their size, bats are the slowest reproducing mammals on Earth. On average, a female rears only one young yearly. These creatures are essential, but since they show up at night and are shrouded in misplaced fear, they rarely get the credit they deserve for their hard work. So, when you see bats emerge at dusk, offer your thanks and reflect on your unseen talents too.

"If the bat has come up for you, it may be time to embrace the healing power of darkness and awaken the amazing power of your senses."

Ways to Connect with Bats

MEDITATION

Close your eyes and attune to the subtle sounds around you. Imagine using sound and extra sensory perception to move about your environment.

SPECIES STATUS

There are many species of bats throughout the world. Some species, like the flying fox, are threatened and many others are struggling as a result of habitat loss, the use of pesticides, and other forms of human impact.

ACTION

If you have an overflow of mosquitoes, try building a bat box so they can live nearby.

NATURE CONNECTION

Learn about the role of bats in your local ecosystem. Can you spot them flying to catch their prey? Go outside at dusk and watch their incredible behavior.

Research and draw
the different flowers
pollinated by the bat,
to produce the fruit
we like to eat. When
you eat a mango
or use agave as a
sweetener, imagine
the bats that helped
them grow.

INNER EXPLORATION

Do you feel unseen? Would you like credit for something that you feel has been overlooked? If so, write about it until you find ways to communicate how you feel.

DRAGONFLY

Imagination · Vision · Transcendence

Dragonflies have been around for over 300 million years, making them one of the oldest living insect species in the world. When dragonflies hatch from their eggs, they are called nymphs and have no resemblance to their adult forms. They live in ponds and marshes, and will shed their skin up to 12 times, depending on the species, and may live as long as four years in this stage. Until one day, they emerge from the water and shed their skin one last time to fly into the sky as an adult dragonfly. In their beautiful new form, they move gracefully and are able to fly up and down, left and right, backward, hover like a helicopter, and catch their prey in midair by grabbing it with their feet.

Most dragonfly species can see colors like ultraviolet light that are beyond human capabilities. With their brilliant iridescent and metallic colors, dragonflies are often associated with dreams and magical realms. In the Chinese practices of *feng shui*, the placing of dragonfly statues in the home is believed to bring new insights and positive change, while in some spiritual traditions the dragonfly acts as a messenger between worlds. Dragonflies are symbols of profound transformation, inspiring us to stay on our path and bring about the changes needed to reach our true potential. If the dragonfly appears, it is time to awaken to your own magic.

"If the dragonfly appears, it is time to awaken to your own magic."

Ways to Connect with Dragonflies

SPECIES STATUS

Dragonflies live on every continent except Antarctica, but the loss of wetland habitats threatens dragonfly populations around the world. The majority of species live in tropical areas and have been little studied. With the destruction of rain forest habitats, many of these species are in danger of becoming extinct before they have even been named. The greatest cause of decline is forest clearance and the consequent drying up of streams and pools which become clogged with silt.

ACTION

Permanent areas of water will attract dragonflies. To encourage female dragonflies to lay eggs in a pond, you may want to grow reeds, lilies, and other aquatic plants to give her a place to perch while laying her eggs.

NATURE CONNECTION

Spend some time near a local pond or lake. Do you see any dragonflies? What colors are they? Sit quietly and watch their fascinating flight patterns and intriguing behavior.

MEDITATION

If you enjoy meditating, try visualizing a dragonfly in one of your practices. Focus on the beauty of their iridescent wings and the magical transformations they are capable of. Tap into their power so you can make the change you need to reach your goals and achieve your dreams.

CREATIVE EXPLORATION

Imagine the world from a
dragonfly's perspective.
What colors can you
see? Where will you go?
Write your story here.

INTERNATIONAL ORGANIZATIONS

1 Animals of the Land

WOLF
Wolf Conservation Center: nywolf.org
Defenders of Wildlife: defenders.org

SNOW LEOPARD
Snow Leopard Trust: snowleopard.org
The Snow Leopard Conservancy:
snowleopardconservancy.org

BLACK BEAR
The Sierra Club: sierraclub.org
Yellowstone to Yukon: y2y.net

ORANGUTAN
Orangutan Foundation International:
orangutan.org
The Orangutan Project:
theorangutanproject.org
Borneo Orangutan Survival: www.
orangutans.com.au

RHINOCEROS
Save the Rhino International:
savetherhino.org
**International Anti-poaching
Foundation:** iapf.org

SPIDER
Union of Concerned Scientists:
ucsusa.org
Bug Life: wildlifetrusts.org

RED SQUIRREL
Trees for Life: treesforlife.org.uk
The Nature Conservancy: nature.org

ELEPHANT
African Wildlife Foundation:
www.awf.org
Save The Elephants:
savetheelephants.org

RED FOX
Save A Fox: Saveafox.com
National Wildlife Federation:
www.nwf.org

SNAKE
Flora and Fauna International:
fauna-flora.org
Advocates for Snake Preservation:
snakes.ngo

2 Animals of the Water

GREAT WHITE SHARK
Project Aware: projectaware.org
Shark Trust: sharktrust.org

HORSE
American Wild Horse Campaign:
americanwildhorsecampaign.org
Return To Freedom:
returntofreedom.org

SEAL
The Ocean Conservancy:
oceanconservancy.org
Pacific Marine Mammal Center:
pacificmmc.org

KOALA
Australian Koala Foundation:
savethekoala.com
Wildlife Warriors: wildlifewarriors.org.au

OCTOPUS
Only One: only.one
Greenpeace: greenpeace.org

PANDA BEAR
Pandas International:
pandasinternational.org
Wildlife SOS: wildlifesos.org

CRAB
Chesapeake Bay Foundation:
www.cbf.org
Acadia Center: acadiacenter.org

TIGER
Panthera Save The Tiger Initiative:
panthera.org/initiative/save-tiger-fund
World Animal Protection:
worldanimalprotection.ca

PLATYPUS
World Wildlife Fund Australia:
wwf.org.au
Global Wildlife Conservation:
globalwildlife.org

Animals of the Water (continued)

MARINE IGUANA
Galapagos Conservancy:
galapagos.org
Oceana: oceana.org

DOLPHIN
National Marine Mammal Foundation:
nmmf.org
Oceanic Preservation Society:
opsociety.org

SEAHORSE
Project Seahorse: projectseahorse.org
Coral Reef Alliance: coral.org

HUMPBACK WHALE
Sea Legacy: sealegacy.org
Sea Shepherd: seashepherd.org

TREE FROG
The Rainforest Alliance:
rainforest-alliance.org
Wildlife Conservation Network:
wildnet.org

Sea Otter
Sea Otter Foundation:
seaotterfoundationtrust.org
Friends of Sea Otters: seaotters.org

TURTLE
Turtle Conservancy:
www.conserveturtles.org
See Turtles: seeturtles.org

3 Animals of the Air

BUTTERFLY
Save Our Monarchs:
saveourmonarchs.org
Xerces Society: www.xerces.org

OWL
National Audubon Society:
www.audubon.org
Urban Bird Foundation: urbanbird.org

EAGLE
Earth Justice: www.earthjustice.org
World Bird Sanctuary:
worldbirdsanctuary.org

HUMMINGBIRD
American Bird Conservancy:
abcbirds.org
Pollinator Partnership: pollinator.org

FIREFLY
Center For Biological Diversity:
www.biologicaldiversity.org
Firefly Conservation and Research:
firefly.org

BUMBLEBEE
Bumblebee Conservation Trust:
bumblebeeconservation.org
The Bee Conservancy:
thebeeconservancy.org

RAVEN
Natural Resources Defense Council:
nrdc.org
Bird Note: birdnote.org

ALBATROSS
The Oceanic Society:
oceanicsociety.org
All About Birds: www.allaboutbirds.org

BAT
Bat Conservation International:
batcon.org
Bats Queensland: batsqld.org.au

DRAGONFLY
The Wilderness Society: www.
wilderness.org
Integral Ecology Research Center:
iercecology.org

GLOSSARY

Here is a select list of words and terms used in this book. I encourage you to look up any other words or phrases that are new to you.

Apex predator
An animal at the top of a food chain without natural predators.

Arachnid
A class of animals that includes spiders, scorpions, mites, and ticks.

Baleen whale
Whales with baleen plates in their upper jaw which are used to filter the small crustaceans they feed on out of large quantities of seawater.

Biodiversity
The variety of life that can be found on Earth, such as plants, animals, fungi, and microorganisms, as well as the communities that they form and the habitats they live in.

Chrysalis
A moth or butterfly at the stage of development when they are covered by a hard case; before they become an adult with wings.

Cosmology
A philosophical, religious, or mythical explanation of the nature and structure of the Universe.

Ecology
The relationships of living creatures to their environments and each other.

Ecological steward
Mindful participation in and protection of the natural environment through conservation and regenerative practices to enhance ecosystem resilience and wellbeing for all creatures.

Estuary
A partially enclosed body of water with a connection to the open sea, and one or more rivers or streams flowing into it.

Exoskeleton
A rigid external covering for the body in some invertebrate animals that provides both support and protection.

Herbivore
An animal that feeds solely on plants.

Hibernation
The condition or period of time that an animal or plant spends in a dormant state during winter.

Insectivore
A plant or animal that feeds primarily on insects.

Invertebrate
An animal or insect that has no spinal column.

Keystone species
A species whose presence and role within an ecosystem has a profound effect on other organisms within the system.

Limbic system
Part of the brain involved in behavioral and emotional responses, especially when it comes to survival: feeding, reproduction and caring for young, and fight-or-flight responses.

Mangroves
A salt-tolerant shrub or small tree that grows in coastal saline or brackish water.

Metamorphosis
The process of transformation from an immature form to an adult form in two or more distinct stages.

Microalgae
Unicellular species found in freshwater and marine systems, living in both the water column and sediment. They exist individually or in groups and are capable of performing photosynthesis.

Nymphs
Immature forms of insects such as dragonflies that do not change greatly as they grow.

Sagacity
Having wisdom or far-sighted, clear judgment.

Syngnathid fish
The only animal family in which the males, not the females, carry their young.

Ubiquitous
Something that is everywhere and constantly encountered.

Ultraviolet light
Beyond the violet light that is visible to humans in terms of frequency, wavelength, and energy. Many animals such as some insects, some reptiles, crocodiles, salamanders, and small birds can see things that reflect this light.

Zero waste
Responsible production, consumption, reuse, and recovery of products so that there is no harmful impact on land, water, or air, or on plant and animal health.

Index

A

actions 13
activities 13
acute perception 174–177
adaptability 54–57, 110–112
affection 70–74, 132–134
air, animals of the 140–183
albatross 11, 170–172
    organizations 187
ancient wisdom 48–51
apex predator (definition) 188
arachnid (definition) 188
athleticism 44–47
attraction 162–164
awareness 118–120

B

balance 76–78, 90–94
baleen whale (definition) 188
bat 11, 174–177
    organizations 187
biodiversity (definition) 188
black bear 10, 26–29
    organizations 184
bumblebee 11, 162–164
    organizations 187
butterfly 11, 142–145
    organizations 187

C

change 142–145
characteristics, animal 10–11
chrysalis (definition) 188
comfort 70–74
communication 114–117
compassion 114–117
confidence 80–82, 150–153,
    166–169
connect, ways to 12–13
consciousness 122–127
cooperation 48–51, 114–117,
    132–134

cosmology (definition) 188
crab 10, 100–105
    organizations 185
creativity 40–42

D

dedication 66–68
depth 110–112
devotion 162–164
dignity 80–82
dolphin 11, 114–117
    organizations 186
dragonfly 11, 180–183
    organizations 187
drawing 13
dreamwork 13

E

eagle 11, 150–153
    organizations 187
ecological steward (definition)
    188
ecological stewardship 6, 16–18
ecology (definition) 188
elegance 22–24
Elephant 10
organizations 184
elephant 48–51
elusiveness 22–24
endurance 66–68, 170–172
energy 44–47
enigmatic 106–109
esoteric wisdom 166–169
estuary (definition) 188
exoskeleton (definition) 188

F

family 16–18
firefly 11, 158–160
    organizations 187
focus 86–88

G

glossary 188–189
grace 66–68

great white shark 10, 86–88
    organizations 185
groundedness 36–38

H

harmony 76–78
herbivore (definition) 188
hibernation (definition) 188
horse 10, 66–68
    organizations 185
hummingbird 11, 154–156
    organizations 187
humpback whale 11, 122–127
    organizations 186
hunger 86–88

I

imagination 180–183
Indigenous cultures 6
ingenuity 54–57, 96–99
initiation 174–177
inner exploration 13
inner knowing 146–149
inner spark 158–160
inner voice 90–94
insectivore (definition) 188
intelligence 54–57
intensity 150–153
introspection 26–29
intuition 96–99
invertebrate (definition) 189

J

joy 154–156

K

key words 10–11
keystone species (definition)
    189
kindness 48–51
koala 10, 70–74
organizations 185

L

land, animals of the 14–83

letting go 142–145
limbic system (definition) 189
longing 90–94
loyalty 170–172

M
magic 158–160
mangroves (definition) 189
marine iguana 11, 110–112
    organizations 186
meditation 12
meditative stillness 110–112
metamorphosis (definition) 189
microalgae (definition) 189
mindfulness 12, 136–138
movement 12
mystery 96–99, 122–127,
166–169

N
nature connection 13
navigation 146–149
new beginnings 128–130
nurturing 26–29
nymphs (definition) 189

O
octopus 10, 96–99
organizations 185
orangutan 10, 30–35
    organizations 184
organizations 184–187
owl 11, 146–149
    organizations 187

P
panda bear 10, 76–78
    organizations 185
partnership 118–120, 170–172
patience 40–42, 118–120
peace 30–32
perception, acute 174–177
perspective 150–153
platypus 11, 106–109
    organizations 185

play 132–134
power 80–82
predator, apex (definition) 188
preparedness 44–47
presence 30–32, 146–149
protection 100–104

R
radiance 154–156
raven 11, 166–169
    organizations 187
rebirth 60–64, 174–177
receptivity 40–42
red fox 10, 54–59
    organizations 184
red squirrel 10, 44–47
    organizations 184
relentlessness 86–88
remembrance 154–156
renewal 60–64
rhinoceros 10, 36–39
    organizations 184
rhythm 100–104

S
sacred space 76–78
sagacity 136–138
sagacity (definition) 189
sea otter 11, 132–134
    organizations 186
seahorse 11, 118–120
    organizations 186
seal 10, 90–94
    organizations 185
sensitivity 100–104
sensory exploration 13
slowing down 136–138
snake 10, 60–64
    organizations 184
snow leopard 10, 22–25
    organizations 184
solitude 30–32
song 128–130

soul song 122–127
species status and awareness
    12
specificity 70–74
spider 10, 40–43
    organizations 184
stillness, meditative 110–112
strength 22–24
sweetness 162–164
syngnathid fish (definition) 189

T
tenacity 36–38
tiger 10, 80–83
    organizations 185
tranquility 36–38
transcendence 60–64, 180–183
transformation 128–130
tree frog 11, 128–130
    organizations 186
trust 142–145
turtle 11, 136–138
    organizations 186

U
ubiquitous (definition) 189
ultraviolet light (definition) 189
unique 106–109
unpredictable 106–109

V
vision 180–183

W
waste, zero (definition) 189
water, animals of the 84–139
wildness 16–18
wisdom, esoteric 166–169
wolf 6, 10, 16–21
    organizations 184
wonder 158–160
writing 13

Z
zero waste (definition) 189

Dedication

To the wild creatures of the land,
water, and air. May we humans come
to our senses and remember
that we are all related.

To Ebony, Toby, Kobe, and Daphne;
I couldn't have asked for better
canine teachers and friends.

And finally, to Atka, beloved Arctic
wolf. May the ripple effect of your life
and work dissolve misunderstanding
and set your species free.